# GRACE

*The essence of God*

# GRACE

*The essence of God*

Wayne Monbleau

**LOVING GRACE PUBLICATIONS**
**BOX 531, LANCASTER, NH 03584**

LOVING GRACE PUBLICATIONS
BOX 531, LANCASTER, NH 03584

Front Cover Photograph:
"Sunrise on Mount Desert Island" by Wayne Monbleau

Back Cover Photograph: John Jaworowski

All Scripture quotations from the New American Standard Bible,
© The Lockman Foundation 1960, 1962, 1963, 1968, 1971, 1972,
1973, 1975, except where otherwise noted.

ISBN 0-944648-05-3

# CONTENTS

# Introduction

*"By the grace of God I am what I am."*

*1st Corinthians 15:10*

Look at the above verse. Is this your truth? Are you what you are by the grace of God?

To so many Christians, this verse is merely a doctrinal fact which reminds them of the method of their salvation. "God's unmerited favor" is the automatic response of many a believer when asked what grace is.

Is this, in fact, all that grace is, a theological footnote to be fit in with all the other data of our faith?

What would you do if you woke up one morning to discover that during the night someone had removed every reference about God's love from your Bible? What type of God would you be left with? Would you go on as if nothing had happened or would you be outraged that someone had done such a thing?

I give this example to you because the church, for the most part, has effectively removed the grace of God from our lives simply by ignoring its existence. I encounter thousands of believers every year through my radio counselling ministry who have no actual idea as to what grace truly is and as to its centrality to the Christian life. To them grace is little more than something said before dinner.

You wouldn't let someone remove God's love from your life, and I'm sure that after reading this book you will know the absolute importance of grace to your life as well.

Grace is not some dry doctrinal observation to be assimilated with the rest of our head knowledge. Grace is the heart of everything God is and has done for us. Grace is the essence of real life. It's the personification of the abundant life Jesus promised us. By the grace of God, we are what we are. This *is* truth, whether we realize it or not.

I trust this book will be used of our Lord Jesus Christ to bring you into the revelation and realization of the true nature of God, the Lord who now lives His life in you. "Christ in you, the hope of glory" (Colossians 1:27) will become your ever present reality as grace is magnified in your own heart.

This is a journey into a heart relationship. We must pass out of our outer external concepts of God, for grace will never be real to the one who bases his life upon his own performance, works, efforts, and talents. But, to the one who truly desires to know the essence of God in his own heart of hearts, grace will be realized as the very center from which all life issues forth. The innermost man, the spirit of the man within him where Christ resides, will at last come forth into the sunshine to guide us into all the truth as we see Jesus revealed in grace.

It's as Paul wrote in the third chapter of Colossians, "When Christ, who is our life, is revealed, then you also will be revealed with Him in glory" (3:4). This is not a reference to the second coming. It is, in fact, the only way in which we can see Him as He is and consequently ourselves, as we are in our new creations.

Grace *is* the essence of God. May this book bring you into the full awareness of Christ, who is our life.

Wayne Monbleau
October 3, 1983
Lancaster, NH

# Chapter 1

# The Definition of Grace

*"For you know the grace of our Lord Jesus Christ, that though He was rich, yet for your sake He became poor, that you through His poverty might become rich."*

**2nd Corinthians 8:9**

What is grace?

The most frequently quoted definition is, "God's unmerited favor". This is certainly true, for we know the Bible tells us all have sinned and fallen short of the glory of God and therefore all deserve death (Romans 3:23 & 6:23). Yet God, rich in mercy, extends His life to us in the only way out of our hopeless dilema. When we accept His invitation to life through Jesus Christ, grace becomes the only possible explanation for God's action. He grants us life in Him, an abundant and forever life. We who were doomed under the curse of sin and death are gloriously set free from our bondage into the kingdom of the Son.

Do we deserve this release from darkness to light, from death to life? No. Then why does He do this for us? The answer is really quite simple and it is also the most profound fact the world will ever hear. God grants us life because He loves us and in His act of love the word, grace, is born.

Grace truly is God's unmerited favor. We will never come to a place through our works where we will be able to prove we are worthy of the grace in salvation God has so freely given us. We will forever be in the position of realizing that apart from grace, we would be lost, empty, and lifeless.

Yes, grace is God's unmerited favor but, grace is also much more than that. The Bible actually gives us the true definition of grace. As we look at the following Scripture together I hope you will see the depth and meaning it holds for us. I pray you will receive a revelation of the centrality of God's grace to all true living. I hope you will yield yourself to His grace, for we are about to see that grace is Jesus Christ!

In his second letter to the Corinthian church, Paul wrote, "For you know the grace of our Lord Jesus Christ, that though He was rich, yet for your sake He became poor, that you through His poverty might become rich" (8:9).

What is grace? What is the true Biblical definition of grace? Grace is Jesus Christ giving up all He had in glory, as God, and coming to this planet to purposely become the most mistreated person who ever lived. Why did He do this? He did it because He wanted you to have all of His riches and wealth. His suffering long agony upon the cross at Calvary was His act of becoming our poverty, paying our penalty of death, in order to transfer His abundance to us. He became poor so we might be rich.

Grace is Jesus paying for your sins for no other reason than the fact that He loves you and wants to give you everything He has. Grace is Jesus taking your poverty and giving you His riches. Grace is Jesus saying, "I love My creation and will gladly sacrifice

My life to bridge the gap between man and Me".

Grace is Jesus Christ! It's His love for you long before you knew Him, His willingness to come to earth, His life, death, resurrection, and His unmatchable invitation for all to know Him personally as Savior and Lord.

Grace is much more than a simple statement of God's unmerited favor. Grace, in its very depth, is nothing less than a revelation of the heart of our Lord Jesus Christ.

This is why grace is absolutely central in my relationship with God. This is why I cannot listen to anybody who tries to present Christianity as a "what you do for God to earn His favor" type of religion. Any doctrine or belief which seeks to add our efforts in any way to God's grace is an insult to Jesus' love for us. Any so-called Christianity which is not based *and lived* upon grace is not a true Christianity at all!

Grace is not some nice sounding spiritual concept to be assimilated with all other Bible knowledge. Grace is the essence of our life in Christ.

Thank God for His grace. Pray for sight to truly see what grace means to you personally.

Jesus gave up all He had because He loves you. Don't you want to know this love? Look unto Jesus. Fix your eyes upon Him, as the epistle of Hebrews says (12:2), and His grace will be ever increasing to you.

# Chapter 2

# The Fullness and Glory of God

*"We beheld His glory, glory as of the only begotten from the Father, full of grace and truth." "For of His fullness we have all received, and grace upon grace."*

***John 1:14,16***

Do you know the fullness of God? Can you honestly say you personally experience His fullness in your own life?

To be in the fullness of God means you would be full of His blessings, full of His presence, full of His promises, and full of His love. In your relationship with Him, fullness would mean you realize all is yours in Jesus Christ.

What about His glory? Can you tell me you see and experience the glory of God daily in your life?

There are not many examples from the Bible of people who have seen the glory of God and yet I tell you, every born again believer is entitled to know, feel, see, and live in God's glory. Before I show you why I believe this, let's look together into the life of one who actually did see the glory of the Lord.

In the 33rd chapter of the book of Exodus we are given an account of the time when Moses asked to see God's glory. It's not so much that Moses was the only one God would let Himself get close to, as it was that Moses was the only one willing to get close to God. Remember, earlier on in the book of Exodus, this is what the people said to Moses, "Speak to us yourself and we will listen; but let not God speak to us, lest we die" (20:19). You see, they had a warped perspective of God, born out of a distant relationship, and they allowed their decisions to be formed through their ignorance rather than through the true knowledge of God.

So when Moses asked to see God's glory, he was the only one asking simply because he was the only one drawing near to God. I believe if the people of Isreal had been willing to be led by a real knowledge of God, instead of by their fears, then everyone would have been asking to see the glory of God.

As it was though, Moses was the only one asking. The Lord's reply to Moses' request was, "I Myself will make all My goodness pass before you." He also said, "While My glory is passing by, I will put you in the cleft of the rock and cover you with My hand until I have passed by" (33:19,22).

And so, Moses beheld the glory of God. This passage of Scripture from Exodus makes it seem like it was a very unusual thing for someone to see God's glory. It makes it appear like *we* would never stand a chance of ever having such a glorious experience in our life time. Well, it was unusual, and it was rare, and it was special, but I want you to know it's also for you.

How can I say this? It may sound sacreligious to some for me to say such a thing. Let me make it even more fantastic. Moses beheld God's glory once as far as we know. What I'm saying is you can behold this same magnificent glory every day!

Don't forget about my first question either. In addition to God's glory, I believe you can experience His fullness in your own life every day too!

Your question at this point should not be, "Can this really be true for me?" The real question is, does the Bible say this? The answer is yes, this is exactly what the Bible says.

Read these two verses very carefully "We beheld His glory, glory as of the only begotten from the Father, full of grace and truth." "For of His fullness we have all received, and grace upon grace." (John 1:14,16)

According to these verses, how can you, today, see God's glory and receive His fullness? Perhaps I should phrase it another way. What are the characteristics of God's glory and fullness?

God's glory is full of grace and truth, right? So if you want to see His glory, look at grace and truth. God's fullness is grace upon grace, right? So if you want to know His fullness, look at His grace.

The simple point I'm making is this: as you center your life upon the grace of God, you will be placing yourself in a position to know His fullness and see His glory. Now, who wouldn't want to do that? What Christian, in his right mind, would turn down the opportunity to live in God's glory and fullness?

Unfortunately, it does happen. Christians turn down this magnificent opportunity every day. You might say, "I'd never do that. I'd never turn down God's fullness." Good. I hope you never do turn Him down. However, thousands of Christians living right now know nothing of His fullness and glory. Rather than looking at the many possible causes, such as a works mentality, law centeredness, self centeredness, sin centeredness, etc., let's return to the solution.

There is only one place where God's glory and fullness can be seen and experienced, and that is in His grace. Any relationship with God which is not centered, experientially, upon His grace, is a relationship doomed to never realize its full potential.

If you are willing to let God's grace take its rightful place in your own life, then I guarantee you upon the word of God that you will know His overwhelming fullness and glory as reality in your relationship with Him.

"We beheld His glory, glory as of the only begotten from the Father, full of grace and truth." "For of His fullness we have all received, and grace upon grace." Go now, and let God's glory and fullness be the delight of your life.

# Chapter 3

# Grace is a Gift

*"But the free gift is not like the transgression. For if by the transgression of the one the many died, much more did the grace of God and the gift by the grace of the one man, Jesus Christ, abound to the many."*

*Romans 5:15*

*"Gentiles are fellow-heirs and fellow-members of the body, and fellow-partakers of the promise in Christ Jesus through the Gospel, of which I was made a minister, according to the gift of God's grace which was given to me according to the working of His power."*

*Ephesians 3:6&7*

What makes a gift a gift? If I go to the store and purchase a certain thing, can I refer to that object as a gift? If I work hard all day in order to obtain something through my efforts, can I call what I earn a gift? In each case the answer is no. If I purchase or earn something, I cannot refer to that thing as a gift.

There is only one way something can truly qualify as a gift. If I am given something totally apart from any work or payment on my part, then that is a gift. What makes it a gift? The fact that it is given to me freely, without any obligation, is what makes it a gift.

How is it we are given gifts? If we don't pay for them, and if we don't earn them, then what would motivate someone to give us gifts? What's in it for them?

The giver of a gift receives his blessing in the giving. He grants us something of his own, has something he has paid for or has earned, simply out of love.

So, if we are given a gift, it must mean someone loves us. It must mean we are important to somebody.

Are you important to somebody? Is there someone who loves you? According to the Bible, the answer is yes! You are loved! God loves you and cares for you.

His grace, His fullness and glory found in Jesus, is a gift He offers you. Now remember, if it's a gift then you don't work for it and you are not required to pay for it. So, don't respond to my statement of God's grace being a gift, with a remark of how you could never possibly be good enough to earn it. That's not the point. A gift is not given because you are good enough. No. A gift is given because you are loved, and *you* are loved, by God Himself.

Paul's letter to the church at Rome says this, "But the free gift is not like the transgression. For if by the transgression of the one the many died, much more did the grace of God and the gift by the grace of the one man, Jesus Christ, abound to the many" (Romans 5:15).

Paul is speaking about the sin of Adam. Through his transgression we all died, for his sin infected us all. "All have sinned and fall short of the glory of God" (Romans 3:23). However, Paul goes on to say the grace of God, in Jesus, abounds all the more.

How can this be? Because through Jesus' death and resurrection, He defeated sin. When we are born again, our new life is proof of the fact that God's grace is more powerful than sin. So, grace abounds more than sin does. This grace is a gift. It is freely given to us, out of love.

Do you know what is great about God's gifts? They are life changing gifts. They aren't just conversation pieces to be put on some dusty shelf. God's gifts change us. His gifts make us new. His gifts free us from darkness. His gifts place the light of the world within. God's grace is the greatest life changing gift ever made possible to the world, and it's free, so all can come. There is not one person who has ever lived who has not had the opportunity to freely receive the grace of God. Because grace is a gift, it is available to all.

Another verse of Scripture which shows us how the gift of grace changes lives, is found in Paul's letter to the Ephesian church. This time Paul is sharing how God's grace has changed him. He wrote, "Gentiles are fellow-heirs and fellow-members of the body, and fellow-partakers of the promise in Christ Jesus through the Gospel, of which I was made a minister, according to the gift of God's grace which was given to me according to the working of His power" (Ephesians 3:6&7).

What was it that made Paul a minister? Was it a matter of his desire, decision, efforts, or works? No. It was according to the gift of God's grace. The grace of God touched his life, changed him from one who persecuted Jesus to one who preached Jesus, and it all came to him as a gift.

Are you able to see the potential of change and renewing in your own life as you receive this magnificent gift? God is no respector of persons. The same gift of grace which changed Paul so radically is available to you, and is waiting to transform you. Hopefully, you will see, through what I have shared with you in this chapter, that God's gift of grace is for you and requires nothing on your part, except your willingness to receive it.

How would you feel if you lovingly chose a gift for someone very special to you, only to have the gift refused? Wouldn't you feel slighted and hurt? Wouldn't you want to say, "I love you and want you to have this gift. Please don't refuse it"? What if that person responded to you by saying, "I'm not good enough", or "I don't deserve this."? You know that wouldn't matter and you would also know that didn't have anything to do with why you wanted to give the gift in the first place.

I've said all that to say this; don't turn God down. Don't refuse His gift on the grounds of some false humility or unworthiness. Receive His gift in the same spirit in which it is offered, which is love, and you will be happy, blessed, fulfilled, changed, transformed, and you will be allowing God to be fullfilled as well, through your reception of the gift of His grace.

# Chapter 4

# Salvation is By Grace

*"But we believe that we are saved through the grace of the Lord Jesus, in the same way as they also are."* **Acts 15:11**

*"But God, being rich in mercy, because of His great love with which He loved us, even when we were dead in our transgressions, made us alive together with Christ (by grace you have been saved), and raised us up with Him, and seated us with Him in the heavenly places, in Christ Jesus, in order that in the ages to come He might show the surpassing riches of His grace in kindness toward us in Christ Jesus. For by grace you have been saved through faith; and that not of yourselves, it is the gift of God; not as a result of works, that no one should boast."* **Ephesians 2:5-9**

In the 15th chapter of Acts, we are given the account of what the early church did with the Mosaic law concerning new gentile believers. There were those who advocated the attachment and observance of the law for these new converts. This attitude was born out of an ignorance of the full provision under the new covenant. Those who were for the continuation of the law represented the believer who, although he is thankful to God for salvation, is never the less reluctant to part with the old "secure" religious methods. So, he tries to have it both ways, Jesus for salvation and the system for continuation.

The apostles and elders were not going to be taken in by this kind of worldly logic so, they decided to place no burdens upon the new believers except to say they should refrain from things contaminated by idols, from fornication, from what is strangled, and from blood (a point later modified in Paul's first letter to the Corinthians).

In the midst of this discussion, Peter addressed the assembly and at one point said, "But we believe that we are saved through the grace of the Lord Jesus, in the same way as they also are" (Acts 15:11). The context of this passage is of Peter stressing this fact; if we are saved by grace, then it only makes sense we are also kept by grace. In other words, if God's grace has saved us, as we all agree it has, then why are we considering the continuation of a system based upon our own efforts which couldn't even save us in the first place? Thankfully Peter's words prevailed, not because he was personally persuasive, but because he spoke the mind of Christ while others were too busy trying to bring God down to their own level.

Do you realize your salvation is one hundred percent God's grace? I hope for your sake you do know this, for if you think in any way your salvation is grace plus something, whether it be works, law, baptism, or anything else, then you are gravely mistaken. We are saved through the grace of God. His gift of grace to us gives us our salvation, and it can only be a gift if it stands alone, without our adding contingencies to it. Our salvation is contingent upon nothing but the grace of our Lord Jesus.

What is it we are saved from? Have you ever thought about this? First, we are saved from sin (Romans 6:14). We are also saved from death (Hebrews 2:9). We are saved from our own works and efforts (Hebrews 4:10&11, Colossians 2:16-23). And, surprisingly enough, we are saved from the law (Romans 7:4-6, Galatians 3:23-25).

Sin kept us locked up in our own fruitless passions. Death kept us bound up in seperation from God. Our works kept us in a never ending and never successful attempt to win God's approval. And the law kept us apart forever from God, because we could never accomplish its demands.

What a burden! What an incredible pressure cooker we were caught in, and there was no way out. Make no mistake about that. We were lost, without hope, and without escape.

That's why God's grace is so great, because He gave us the freedom we wanted and needed, but could never obtain on our own. His free gift came to us and released us from all these burdens which had trapped us in experiential death for so long.

This is why it is so ridiculous to think salvation is a grace-plus-something proposition. If we truly see our condition outside of Christ, then we will know better than to think somehow God must require effort upon our part in addition to His grace in order for us to be saved. This is also why Peter was so adamant about a one hundred percent by grace salvation.

Here is another Scripture which says it even stronger, "But God, being rich in mercy, because of His great love with which He loved us, even when we were dead in our transgressions, made us alive together with Christ (by grace you have been saved), and raised us up with Him, and seated us with Him in the heavenly places, in Christ Jesus, in order that in the ages to come He might show the surpassing riches of His grace in kindness toward us in Christ Jesus. For by grace you have been saved through faith; and that not of yourselves, it is the gift of God; not as a result of works, that no one should boast" (Ephesians 2:5-9).

This is as straight forward and to the point as Scripture can get. You are saved by grace, and not of yourselves. This means you don't have any part in it. You don't earn it through works. You don't gain it by adherence to the law which you couldn't adhere to even if you tried with all your might. It doesn't come to you through your self atonement for sins. Salvation, your salvation, is by grace and grace alone.

As Ephesians says, there is no ground for boasting when it comes to salvation. If you could boast about your salvation, then that would mean you do play a part in it. But there is no boasting, just thankfulness from our hearts to our loving Lord Jesus.

Do you realize God loves you so much that He has given you a complete salvation dependent totally upon Himself and made available to you through the gift of His grace? Do you see this? The realization of salvation by grace will experientially release you from striving under some false concept of a God-plus-me salvation, which could only keep you bound up and in ignorance of the finished work of Jesus Christ.

Look at God's grace. See your salvation, and thank Him for His great love. He has given us, in Himself, the entrance into eternal and abundant life.

# Chapter 5

# The Only Way Grace Can be Grace

*"But if it is by grace, it is no longer on the basis of works, otherwise grace is no longer grace."*

**Romans 11:6**

In the last chapter I made the rather bold statement that grace is our one hundred percent salvation, and to add anything to God's grace would be to make grace void. You may have wondered why this is so.

In this chapter, we are going to look at a very telling portion of the Scripture which, I am sure, will explain to you why grace cannot be mixed with any other substance and still be called grace.

It's like putting two colors together. If you mix blue with yellow, what do you have? Do you have blue and yellow? No, you have something completely different now called green. In the same way, if you take grace and mix it with some other component, such as the law or works, then you no longer have grace at all.

You have a new substance, and that new substance is called deception, because if grace is a gift how can it be mixed or incorporated with a non-gift substance and still be called a gift?

In order for grace to be grace, it has to stand alone. The addition of anything else contaminates grace and at that point grace ceases to be grace. As I said in an earlier chapter, if you try to pay for a gift, then you no longer have a gift.

You may wonder why anyone would want to add on to the grace of God. To understand the reasoning for such an action, we must first have a clear revelation of our natural or fleshy tendencies.

The whole world operates on the principle of looking out for #1. Along with this comes the ingrained pattern of desiring glory for our successes, as well as shunning the blame onto scapegoats for our failures.

I'm afraid Christians carry this mentality right into their spiritual lives without even trying. While most everyone is grateful for the salvation procured for them by the Lamb of God, the time soon comes, almost immediately in many cases, where we decide we have to "give God a hand".

Our old flesh has a built in revulsion to grace, because if it's all grace then we cannot boast or take any credit. So, instead of receiving grace for our whole lives, we limit it to salvation and then construct an elaborate new system which may differ from group to group but basically says "God's power is dependent upon my efforts". The flesh rejoices because it once again can take credit for successes, and we go merrily along, publicly saying it's all God and privately relishing our great knowledge and power.

However, any addition to grace completely eradicates the power of grace in our lives. The fact so many Christians don't even miss grace is a strong testament to our desire of trying to perfect ourselves after the flesh (Galatians 3:3). As you can see, Satan's original sin of independence from God is very much alive and well within the ranks of born again believers everywhere.

Grace means an utter dependence upon God, one in which there is simply no room for the flesh to connive its way back onto the throne of our hearts. The Christian repentance-obedience-works ethic is just a thinly veiled attempt at placing Adam as king of Christianity.

Romans 11:6 puts it this way, "But if it is by grace, it is no longer on the basis of works, otherwise grace is no longer grace."

I hope you see the importance of what is being said here. Beware of anyone or anything which attempts to eradicate grace by the introduction of some other system, whether it be pertaining to salvation, growth, or any of God's blessings. Most likely, an individual would never admit to doing such a thing. The approach would be more subtle like, "Yes, I agree we are saved by grace, but we prove our acceptance through the law and our works." In light of what I've already shared, do you see the flaw in this argument? Remember, if grace is a gift, then you don't need to prove a thing. You just gladly receive the gift.

Now, to be sure, as we grow in Christ, our growth will find outward expression through good works. But these works are a *result* of God's grace touching our lives, and are in no way connected to our obtaining grace.

You see, the problem is, Christians don't have much faith in God's grace these days. It is common to hear someone make the statement, "Oh, brother Wayne, if you preach grace people are going to think they can go out and sin and it will be alright." Where do these accusations come from? Certianly not from the

Bible. As we will see later on in this book, grace is not freedom to sin. On the contratry, grace is the only freedom *from* sin. It's just a case of people refusing to entrust themselves fully into God's care, so they devise elaborate "grace plus" formulas. These formulas may differ, depending upon whatever favorite laws or works a preacher advocates. But the end result is still the same: grace is mixed and therefore is no longer grace at all.

Are you willing to trust God's gracious gift fully in your own life? Are you willing to take a stand to refuse any compromising of the grace of God? If you are willing, then you will be embarking upon the most exciting journey life has to offer. A one hundred percent trust in God's power will place you in the position to be knowing God's miracles and provision in your own daily walk with Christ.

Thank God again for His precious gift, and remember this gift can only remain in its power if it is allowed to stand alone. Grace is only grace when it is all grace. Any addition to grace, and grace will cease to be grace.

# Chapter 6

# Freedom From Sin

*'Sin shall not be master over you, for you are not under law, but under grace.'*

*Romans 6:14*

Sometimes I wonder if other preachers have the same Bible I have. I listen to some of the strangest things when I hear various teachers, and the subject of freedom from sin is one of the most distorted of all Biblical truths being taught today.

The usual line preached goes something like this: "Brother, if you want to be free from sin, then you had better consecrate yourself to the Lord and walk after all of His laws. God's law is our boundary to protect us from falling into sin." Have you ever heard this approach before? You probably have in one way or another and the really sad thing is, most people who hear this type of reasoning usually nod their heads in fervent agreement.

Let's get right to the heart of it, in Scripture. God's law won't keep you from sin. The startling truth is; God's law keeps you bound up in sin! How can I say this? Well, it's not me saying it. The Bible repeatedly says this.

First Corinthians 15:56 says, "The power of sin is the law." According to this verse, where does sin derive its power from? The law, that's where its power is. The third chapter of Romans tells us why this is so. "Now we know that whatever the law says, it speaks to those who are under the law, that every mouth may be closed, and all the world may become accountable to God" (3:19). The law speaks so every mouth may be closed and all the world may become accountable to God. Did you read that? How can this be?

Perhaps I should say here God's law is just, holy, and good. God's law is right. There is not one thing wrong or out of place in God's law. But here is what the next verse in this chapter of Romans tells us: "Because by the works of the law no flesh will be justified in His sight; for through the law comes the knowledge of sin" (verse 21).

You see, God's law is right, but there is one big flaw with the whole system of the law. The law is right, but we aren't. The law is God's word, but we can't obey it and the result is, through the law comes the knowledge of our sin. Our failure to consistently meet the demands of the law only makes us aware of sin and failure. You can preach the law until you are blue in the face, but there is only one possible outcome to that kind of message; defeat and sin consciousness.

You may be wondering at this point that if this is so, then why did God institute the law in the first place? Here is the reason why He brought the law into being: He wanted us to know we could not meet its demands. In his letter to the Galatians, Paul put it this way: "But before faith came, we were kept in custody under the law, being shut up to the faith which was later to be revealed. Therefore the law has become our tutor to lead us to Christ, that we may be justified by faith. But now that faith has come, we are no longer under a tutor" (Galatians 3:23-25).

Why was the law given?—To lead us to Christ. As we have seen, the law makes us aware of sin. Thus, sin's power is found in the law. The reason why God does it this way is so we will see our need for a Savior. As this portion of Scripture tells us, when we do come to Christ we are justified by faith and are no longer under the tutor. When a person comes to Christ, the work of the law is done. It's usefulness is over.

To continue under this tutor as a Chrsitian is to ignore Jesus Christ. It's putting yourself right back under the very power of sin.

Whatever happened to the law anyway? The Bible tells us Jesus fulfilled the law and the law becomes fulfilled in us when we receive Christ as Savior. "The law of the spirit of life in Christ Jesus has set you free from the law of sin and death. For what the law could not do, weak as it was through the flesh, God did: sending His own Son in the likeness of sinful flesh and as an offering for sin, He condemned sin in the flesh, in order that the requirement of the law might be fulfilled in us, who do not walk according to the flesh, but according to the Spirit" (Romans 8:2-4). This section of Scripture, perhaps more than any other, shows us how the law and sin were, and are, interwoven. Moreover, we see that the reason why Jesus died for us was to condemn sin in His flesh, referring to His death, so the requirement of the law might be fulfilled.

Think about this: if something is fulfilled, do we still need to do it? If it's fulfilled, then it's finished, right? We can go on to something else now because the law is finished. We can walk in the full provision of the New Covenant in Jesus Christ, for He has fulfilled the law, met all of its demands, and it is fulfilled in us who believe.

Can't you see that saying the law keeps you from sin is a total misunderstanding and the cruelest of all teachings to give to a Christian? The law doesn't keep you from sin, it keeps you in sin. Its demands only make you aware of your failures. I tell you, there is a better way. See what Jesus has done, walk in His finished work, and you will be experientially free from sin.

Here is where grace comes in, because this fantastic blessing of being free from sin is made available to you through the grace of God. Look at this next verse closely. "Sin shall not be master over you, for you are not under law, but under grace" (Romans 6:14). As long as you try to live under the law, sin will be master over you. But if you will accept the truth of grace, then sin will not be master over you. The good news is; you can be free from sin as you live in God's grace.

You see, grace is stronger than the law. The law just said, "Do this and you will live. Don't do this and you will die." But grace says, "Jesus has done it all and He now offers His victory to you freely." Grace is stronger because we don't play a part in it. We have been, and always will be, the weak link in the chain. So, in grace we see Jesus doing for us what we could never do for ourselves and He includes us in His victory.

Another Scripture which expresses this truth is Romans 5:20: "And the law came in that the transgression might increase; but where sin increased, grace abounded all the more." Simple translation: Grace is stronger than sin, for Jesus, who is our grace, defeated sin at the cross.

Isn't it great to know that as you live as a Christian you can keep your eyes on Jesus Christ and be free from sin? Isn't it great to realize that you don't need to carry the burden of the law through each day, but instead you can praise God for fulfilling the law? Isn't it great to have God's grace?

Let me ask you a simple question, one which will let you know where you stand concerning freedom from sin. When you stumble and sin, what are you aware of, your failure or God's covering?

If you become fixed upon your failure, then you must still be caught up with the false concept of thinking the law frees you from sin. As long as you try to follow God by attempting to obey all the laws, I can guarantee you a life of failure and self condemnation. Under that system, every fall you have will only further highlight the great gap between God's word and your performance. You will continually be feeling you ought to be able to do better and will probably condemn yourself for not beating whatever particular sin it is that trips you up. Moreover, after awhile you'll begin to feel like the boy plugging the hole in the dyke; you put your thumb in one hole and three more holes pop out.

God's law can only make you aware of your sin. You'll never get beyond the stage of sin consciousness as long as you continue under the law.

However, if you learn to walk in God's grace, then each fall will put you in contact with His great forgiveness and covering. It's not that you will ignore sin or make little of it, but you will now be in touch with God's perspective rather than your own. The truth of First John will become your reality: "If we confess our sins, He is faithful and righteous to forgive us our sins and to cleanse us from all unrighteousness" (1:9). Instead of being frozen by guilt and frustration at your point of failure, you will be experientially free from the power of sin.

Let's face it, the sin itself lasts only a moment, but the guilt we and others put on ourselves for our sins lasts a life time. The truth is that as long as you measure your performance by the law, that's how long you will feel like a spiritual flop. Or worse, you may run the risk of hardening your heart so you won't feel the guilt. Or maybe you will brush your sins under the rug by focusing on other people's sins. You see, this whole system of trying to perfect oneself by the law is corrupt and your continuation under it can only harm you.

Under grace, you realize you *are* free from sin. Sins paralizing after effects are gone. Now if you fall, you can simply agree with God about your sin, receive His forgiveness, and move on.

Remember, the Scripture also said we would be cleansed. Forgiveness is for the sin itself, whereas cleansing is for the debilitating guilt which always follows our sin. Grace will make you aware of God's power and covering. If you can see God's forgiveness, cleansing, and covering, you will be free to rise up and see your sins conquered.

As you read this, you may be feeling inside like this sounds too easy. Maybe you feel that God shouldn't let you off the hook. Don't you see how deeply ingrained within us is the concept which says we need to pay for our sins? As Christians we do a slight variation on this tune. We can't escape the fact of Jesus paying for our sins. We know He died for the sins of the world, so we no longer say we need to pay for our sins. We remove the phrase "pay for sins" and we substitute "feel guilty for sins". But it's still the same thing, no matter what you choose to call it. You still find yourself suffering for your sins.

There is no condemnation for those in Christ Jesus (Romans 8:1). Stop whipping yourself with guilt and condemnation. Stop this masochistic practice of comparing your failures with God's law. Stop listening to those whose only desire is to point out your faults and short comings. It's time to jettison the false doctrine of victory through obedience to the law. It's time to see Jesus. As we saw earlier, the power of sin is in the law. I hope by this point you truly know this.

Grace is the only true freedom from sin. Those who oppose grace and who are still laboring under the concept of works, will say those who teach grace are encouraging license, freedom *to* sin. This is simply not true.

I'm not saying it's ok to sin. But let's be honest enough with ourselves, and with God. Let's clear the air with the honest confession that we sin. What are we going to do about it?

You can go on condeming yourself and others if you really want to, or you can say, "Let's stop the games and get down to the business of finding true victory over our sins."

Do you think God expects you to come to the point in this life where you will never sin anymore? Once again, that thinking comes from having a law mentality. The truth is, God is not interested in your performance. He is waiting for you to come to the place where you will get sick of your works and will finally turn with the eyes of faith to behold His mighty power working within you. It's His performance, not yours, that God is interested in. We really need to break loose of this death grip that a sin mentality puts us in and instead become fixed in a Christ consciousness. This is where victory is. God has done it and grace is the door to a true spiritual realization of it.

If you continue to make sin the issue, then you will continue to miss the New Covenant truth of the Gospel. But if you will fix your eyes upon the Author and Finisher of your faith, Jesus

Christ, then you will finally begin to perceive real life and victory. Once you learn to place the responsibility where it belongs, with God, then you will be free from the prison house of self. At this point you will truly know what it means to be a joint heir with Jesus. Victory over sin will be *real* in time and space.

So, the next time you fall and stumble, don't look at your failure. Turn from your sin to Jesus and the floodgates of forgiveness, cleansing, and freedom will be opened to you.

Grace is the only true freedom from sin. Grace points us away from ourselves and to our Lord Jesus. "Sin shall not be master over you, for you are not under law, but under grace."

# Chapter 7

# Justification

*"Being justified as a gift by His grace through the redemption which is in Jesus Christ."*

**Romans 3:24**

*"Being justified by His grace we might be made heirs according to the hope of eternal life."*

**Titus 3:7**

In the last chapter I shared two Scriptures with you which speak of justification. The first said, "By the works of the law no flesh will be justified in His sight", and the other told us, "The law has become our tutor to lead us to Christ, that we may be justified by faith" (Romans 3:20, Galatians 3:24). We see from these verses that there was no way under the law we could ever have justification. Instead, as we are told, justification comes through faith.

What is justification? What does it mean to be justified? The Greek word used for justification in the Bible is dik-ah-yŏ-o, and its definition is: to render just or innocent, to free, to justify, and to be made righteous.

Innocent, free, and righteous; these are three words I'm sure all Christians long to know experientially in their own lives. The truth contained in the word justification tells us we can indeed realize these qualities in our hearts when we come to Jesus for salvation. Justification is given to us at the time of our new birth and entrance into God's family.

How would you like to be innocent? You know, in Jesus you really are! It's true. The only problem I have found in my counselling ministry is that people just have an extremely hard time being able to accept this fact. After all, how can you be innocent when you know you have sinned? The Bible says all have sinned, therefore all are guilty, not innocent. Yes, but don't forget about what Jesus accomplished for you when He paid for your sin. His cleansing power is so great, that not only do you receive forgiveness for all your sins, but you also are made innocent. The sin is removed completely from you, as if you had never sinned in the first place. You are made that clean in Jesus!

The Bible says in First John, "My little children, I am writing these things to you that you may not sin. And if anyone sins, we have an advocate with the Father, Jesus Christ the righteous; and He Himself is the propitiation for our sins; and not for ours only, but also for those of the whole world" (2:1&2).

Jesus Christ is your advocate, or lawyer. God the Father is the Judge. And of course, Satan is the accuser of the brethren. You and I are the defendants standing on trial, and what's worse is we know we are guilty of the sins we are accused of.

Let's go into this court room drama.

SATAN: Judge, see those filthy sinners over there? They are guilty of all kinds of terrible things. Why, just last night . . .

JESUS: Your Honor, My clients plead guilty to all charges. But I have paid, in full, for all their sins.

THE FATHER: Where is the payment?

JESUS: I am the payment. My blood poured out at Calvary has paid for the sins of the world. I have assumed responsibility for their actions, and I have taken all their guilt upon Myself.

THE FATHER: In light of these circumstances, there is only one verdict I can reach: NOT GUILTY. I declare the defendants completely innocent, and free of all charges made now and forever.

—CASE CLOSED—

Although I used a court room for illustration, this is in fact what happened in Heaven. Jesus' shed blood atoned, or paid for, all your sins. Past, present, and future sins were paid for in full by our Prince of Peace and you were declared completely innocent.

When God looks at you, He doesn't see your faults, weaknesses, and sins. He sees His child; clean, free, and righteous. If you will truly accept this fact, then you will have the door open in your own life to be able to see yourself in the same way God sees you.

What's more, according to the definition of justification, not only are you made innocent and free by Jesus, but you are also made righteous. It's as if in His covering of all your sins, His own nature became indelibly marked upon you.

Let me emphasize this point: innocence, freedom, and righteousness are not qualities you strive or work for. They are given to you through justification in Jesus Christ.

How do you receive justification? In Romans 3:24, the Scripture says, "Being justified as a gift by His grace through the redemption which is in Jesus Christ."

At the start of this chapter, we saw a verse which stated we are justified by faith. Now we see what our faith is to be placed in; the gift of grace in Jesus Christ. Jesus secured justification for us when He died at the cross and He makes justification available to us through the free gift of His grace.

Another word on our justification by grace is found in Paul's letter to Titus. "But when the kindness of God our Savior and His love for mankind appeared, He saved us, not on the basis of deeds which we have done in righteousness, but according to His mercy, by the washing of regeneration and renewing by the Holy Spirit, whom He poured out upon us richly through Jesus Christ our Savior, that being justified by His grace we might be made heirs according to the hope of eternal life" (3:4-7).

There is still another blessing for us; a result of being justified by grace. In our justification , we are made heirs to the hope of eternal life. God doesn't just give us eternal life, He makes it our possession and birthright. We become heirs.

It is so important and essential for you to recognize your justification in Jesus Christ. You are free. You are innocent. You are righteous. Begin to see yourself in the same way God sees you. There is no bragging or ego involved here; it's just a matter of accepting what the Word of God declares to be truth.

Praise God today that in Him, your case has been decided forever in your favor.

# Chapter 8

# The Essence of Grace

*"The law was given through Moses; grace and truth were realized through Jesus Christ."*                    *John 1:17*

*"But Noah found grace in the eyes of the Lord."*
                    *Genesis 6:8 (King James)*

By the time you reach this chapter, you ought to have a well defined understanding of grace in your own heart. We've seen the definition of grace is Jesus' life, death, and resurrection. We've seen grace is a gift; God's fullness and glory reside in grace; salvation, justification, and freedom from sin are found in grace; and we've also seen grace has to be 100% alone in order to be grace at all. These truths, in addition to a recognition of the importance of grace in your own life, should make you aware of the centrality of grace to true Christianity.

Where is grace? With all you know about the grace of God, can you tell me where you find grace? Paul wrote, in his first letter to the Corinthian church, "I thank my God always concerning you, for the grace of God which was given you in Christ Jesus" (1:4).

Grace is in Christ Jesus. If you are ever in need of grace, look to Jesus. I believe any revelation of the true nature of our Lord will always bring forth grace. The fact is; Jesus is the what, when, why, where, and how of grace.

Can you see from this verse what folly it is to ignore the grace of God? If grace is given to you in Jesus, then to ignore grace is to ignore Jesus. Many of the so called programs or systems of spiritual growth ignore grace entirely and instead put the emphasis right back on you. It all revolves around your works, your adherence to the law, or as the case many times is, your adherence to their laws. Each of these man made systems ignores the truth of the New Covenant provision for your whole life found in the grace of Jesus Christ. You would think anyone who came to Jesus would live by the same grace which had saved him in the first place, but man's ego just can't stand letting God do it all. He has to get himself in there somehow. He realizes he can't save himself, so he tries to make himself, and anybody else, believe he has to keep himself saved. This way old ego can take the credit for maintaining salvation. He may outwardly give God the glory, but deep inside, you, I, and he, know who really is taking the glory.

It's all foolishness. As we are seeing in this book, there is just one way to be saved, and there is just one way to stay saved, and that way is called receiving the grace of God in Christ Jesus.

Well, I suppose the time for the unveiling is here. It's really about time I confessed the absolute truth to you. Grace is in Jesus Christ, and grace is all of the things I mentioned earlier. But that's not the whole truth. You see there is a reason why grace is all this and I might as well tell you now.

The first chapter of John's Gospel says, "The law was given through Moses; grace and truth were realized through Jesus Christ" (1:17). The Greek word used for realized in this verse is "ghin-om-ahee", which means: to cause to be, to become, or to come into being. You see, grace never existed until Jesus existed. Grace did not come into being until Jesus came into being. In other words, grace did not become flesh until the Word became flesh and dwelt among us. Do you see what this means? Grace is found in Jesus Christ, *because grace is Jesus Christ.* Grace is the essence of all Jesus is. The only place grace lives is in Jesus because Jesus is the personification of grace. It is His nature. It's who He is. Now do you see how serious a mistake it is to ignore grace? Do you see what a denial of Christ it is to try to live by anything other than grace?

If you are willing to place your entire life in Jesus Christ right now, then you too will realize grace. Being saved by Jesus, and being kept by Jesus is the only Biblical way to live. Anything else is simply against God's will and is unscriptural.

There is one more verse which I think beautifully expresses the grace found only in Christ Jesus.

In the day of Noah, the world had become absolutely corrupt. It had collectively hardened its heart until it was entirely dead in its sins. Noah, on the other hand, was the only one who loved God and communed with Him.

In the sixth chapter of Genesis, the Lord said to Noah, "I will destroy man whom I have created from the face of the earth; both man, and beast, and the creeping thing, and the fowls of the air; for it repenteth me that I ever made them" (verse 7, King James).

What about Noah? Was his fate to be the same as the rest of

the world? No, for the very next verse says, "But Noah found grace in the eyes of the Lord" (Verse 8, King James). Praise God, Noah was saved. How? By the grace of God, just like everyone else. What I would like to draw your attention to is where Noah found the grace of God. "Noah found grace in the eyes of the Lord." Noah walked with God and loved Him. When he heard about the coming destruction of the world I'm sure he was anxiously awaiting God's word concerning him. Don't you think Noah was worried about what was to become of him? But the most beautiful thing here is that God didn't even say a word. Noah looked up into the face of the Lord he loved, and when he saw His eyes, they were full of grace. Can you imagine what it must have been like to see God looking at Noah with His eyes expressing grace? Noah didn't need a word from God. One look into his Lord's eyes was all he needed to tell him he would be safe.

To me, this is the most beautiful example of someone realizing grace in Jesus Christ. What about you? Are you willing to look into your Lord's eyes today and see His grace towards you? Are you willing to cease your striving, to be still and know He is God? Please, if you truly love the Lord, don't turn Him away, Don't ignore Him. Let His heart's desire be met today in you. Come to Him and place your life fully in His grace, in the person of Jesus Christ.

# Chapter 9

# The Riches of Grace

*"In Him we have redemption through His blood, the forgiveness of our trespasses, according to the riches of His grace."*
**Ephesians 1:7**

*"In order that in the ages to come He might show the surpassing riches of His grace in kindness towards us in Christ Jesus."*
**Ephesians 2:7**

When a person begins to live his or her life according to the grace of God, then that person becomes experientially rich. Not rich by the standards of this world system; but rich in the kingdom of God.

There are Christians who will always be in a state of spiritual poverty and that's sad, because the Lord has something much better for them. You might say at this point, "But Wayne, didn't Jesus say 'Blessed are the poor in spirit'?" Yes, He did say that in the Beatitudes and He also said immediately following, "For theirs is the kingdom of heaven." You see, that verse refers to a person who does not know Jesus, comes to the realization of spiritual poverty outside of God, repents, is born again, and is granted the kingdom of heaven. Spiritual poverty is only to be the condition of those outside of the family of God. It certainly isn't intended for a Christian to be in a state of spiritual poverty. So let's get rid of the idea right away that somehow God is going to want His children to be ignorant of their riches in Jesus Christ.

It is not God's will for spiritual poverty to exist in the church. However, it does live in the church on a wide scale, and this is due to a lack of true teaching on God's grace. As long as a Christian tries to live apart from grace, that Christian will live unaware of the riches in our Lord. You may think this a rather bold statement, but it's true.

You are released from spiritual poverty in only one way and that's by receiving the free gift of grace. You can attain spiritual riches in only one way and that's by receiving the free gift of grace. As long as you remain in a works mentality, law mentality, sin mentality, or anything other than a Christ mentality, that's how long you will remain in spiritual poverty.

Imagine an enormous storehouse filled with all of God's riches. There are many doors around this vast treasure chamber, but there is only one door which actually leads into this room. You try a number of these doors, but each one you open reveals nothing more than solid wall. Finally, in exhaustion, you turn to the last door and to your delight it opens giving you a glorious vision of all your riches. The name emblazed on this final door is "Grace". Grace is the only true entrance into God's storehouse.

Ephesians 1:7 says, "In Him we have redemption through His blood, the forgiveness of our trespasses, according to the riches of His grace." Where does our redemption and forgiveness come from? How do we receive such wonderful blessings? The answer is, according to the riches of His grace.

The Greek word for redemption, in addition to meaning salvation and deliverance, also means "the ransom in full". When Jesus died for our sins at Calvary, He was paying, in His own blood, a ransom for our souls, Today we usually hear the word ransom when we read about kidnapping cases in the news. Well, you and I were being held captive by the devil and there was no way out, no way to freedom. What's worse is that we deserved our fate. But our Lord Jesus paid the ransom! He loosed us from the hand of the adversary and we are now free in Christ.

What is sad is that there are many souls who have been gloriously ransomed by the Lord, and yet they are forever doubting it. There are multitudes of Christians who have been given forgiviness, yet they refuse to believe they have been forgiven. Why is this so? It comes as a result of not understanding and living in God's grace. The Christian who spends all of his time condemning himself, because he knows he can't live up to the harsh standards he, or others, set for him, will never see the great forgiveness and redemption which are his. He can't see them as long as his eyes are fixed upon himself. The Christian who is out there furiously working in order to gain ground with God and lay claim to some of His blessings, will never be able to do so because, as we have already seen, you can't earn a gift.

The truth is, God grants us all we need freely through His grace. As you start living in grace you will begin go see all that is yours. The best part is, you will never be able to exhaust your riches in Christ. There will always be more for you to discover as you walk in His grace.

Look at each day as an opportunity to realize your riches in grace. Doesn't that sound exciting? Well, it is, and this is the way we should be living every day.

There is one more verse I would like you to see regarding the subject of our riches in grace. Again in Ephesians, Paul wrote, "In order that in the ages to come He might show the surpassing riches of His grace in kindness towards us in Christ Jesus" (2:7). How long will this process of realizing our riches in grace go on? It will last forever, through all eternity. That's how rich we are in Jesus. It makes perfect sense to me, that if we know it is God's will for us to be seeing our riches in grace through all eternity, then shouldn't we be concentrating on our riches now? In other words, why wait for eternity? Let's enjoy the view now. If given the choice of remaining in spiritual poverty or living in the riches of grace, I sure know what my choice will be, and I trust yours will be the same.

God has left you an inheritance. You are living in His New Testament. Our Lord has given you His will, or testament, and in it are all of His riches. If someone left you a million dollars in their will, you would be excited wouldn't you? You wouldn't be likely to forget about a million dollar inheritance. Well, in Jesus you have been given a will with a lot more than a million dollars. You have been given redemption, salvation, forgiveness, and justification. In fact, you have been given "every spiritual blessing in the heavenly places in Christ" (Ephesians 1:3).

Enter through the door of God's grace into the vast storehouse of your riches in Christ. Let God show you today just how rich you are in Him.

# Chapter 10

# Grace
# Removes Mountains

*"This is the word of the Lord to Zerubbabel saying, 'Not by might nor power, but by My Spirit,' says the Lord of hosts. 'What are you O great mountain? Before Zerubbabel you will become a plain; and he will bring forth the top stone with shouts of "Grace, grace to it!" ' "*
              *Zechariah 4:6&7*

What does a mountain represent in Scripture? Sometimes it is symbolic of communing with God, as when Jesus went to the mountain to pray, or when the Lord spoke through Haggai telling the people to go to the mountain and gather wood to rebuild the temple. But to most Christians a mountain is synonymous with a trial or difficulty.

We all have mountains in our lives. Without exception, we are all faced with some pretty grim looking mountains at one time or another. I'm sure you could probably recall some mountainous problem in your life that, at the time, you never thought you would ever get over. Mountains do tend to eventually pass away, but that thought is usually not much comfort when you are confronted with some gigantic obstacle in your path of life.

When faced with a mountain, our prayer most likely is, "Oh, God, take me over this mountain, or take me around it." We want that mountain to disappear as fast as it can. But this doesn't seem to be God's way, does it? After awhile of fervent prayer, we may tend to get righteously indignant with God if the mountain still remains. We say, "God, don't you love me? Am I not your child? Don't you hear me?"

I have discovered this truth in my walk with the Lord: while God is not the author of the mountains in our lives, He does use them to bring about a deepening maturity in His children. You see, we try everything within our power to remove mountains from our lives, but they remain because God wants us to see something concerning Him in them, and what He wants us to see is; He doesn't require us to remove our mountains. He wants us to trust *Him* to remove the mountains, and He does this by taking us through our trials. He doesn't take us around, over, or under them. He takes us through them.

In our spiritual immaturity, we tend to think we can handle any situation because, after all, we are God's child. This may sound right but it just isn't true. The truth is, as John the Baptist said once concerning Jesus, God wants us to decrease so He may increase (John 3:30). The painful conclusion you will some day come to, if you haven't already is, as you grow you actually become weaker. What do I mean by that? I mean that in reference to the power of your flesh, growing in Christ will reveal to you how worthless your own strength and ideas are. This is actually a great blessing, because the realization of your own weakness will be the very catalist to bring you into a place of dependancy upon the

Lord. So, when you are weak, you will be strong (2nd Corinthians 12:10).

When a mountainous trial looms up in front of you, are you aware of God's overcoming power, or do you fall apart? Do you trust the Lord, or do you try to climb your Everest all by yourself?

Unfortunately, I have seen many a Christian fall into a severe guilt complex as a result of not being able to conquer his mountains. Well meaning believers pounce upon some poor brother in Christ who may be undergoing a time of trial and they say, "Brother, just rebuke that mountain. Exercise your faith and that mountain will disappear. It's not God's will for you to have any problems." While statements like this may have some technical truth to them, they are usually administered in a rather self-righteous and judgmental spirit. So the poor brother tries exercising faith, and if his mountain still remains, he is told he doesn't have enough faith, or there must be some "secret sin" he hasn't confessed to God. You may think things like this wouldn't happen between real Christians, but it happens all the time. Believers, their heads all puffed up with doctrine, leave the compassion and love of Christ in the dust and go forth ministering guilt and condemnation to anyone unfortunate enough to stumble across their path.

Am I saying faith can't remove mountains? No, not at all. As a matter of fact I'm going to be saying in a moment that it is faith which removes our mountains. What I am saying though is that the concept of faith as some self will power won't remove a thing. Our faith has to be directed towards something and, Biblically speaking, our faith is to be in God's grace. Christians who have bought the teaching which says they can command any trial to immediately depart, simply have not been presented with the whole truth. Instead, they have been given what I refer to as a "half of

-43-

the word heresy". They probably have heard some forceful preacher weave together a few choice Scriptures about whatsoever you ask in prayer believing, you have received. Well, it is Scripture, isn't it you might say? It is the word of God, isn't it? What could be wrong with believing it? I'm not saying there is anything wrong with believing it. It is important to know about claiming victory. It is important to be able to get a firm hold on the promises of God. But it is equally important to know about the other side of the truth too. In other words, take the whole chapter of Hebrews 11. Don't just accept the first half about the saints who overcame all their problems by faith. Accept it all. Accept also the second half about the saints who never received what was promised, and whose faith was also just as strong as those who did receive what was promised.

You see, if you are going to experience true growth, you can't be selective about which Scriptures you will believe. You must believe it all, and that means when you study a subject, you don't jump to a "one answer fits all" conclusion based upon a few Scriptures. You study all the Bible has to say, and if the Bible says a few different things on, for example, the way prayer is answered, you don't just choose the one you like best. You take it all, realizing God can work differently in each situation. After all, we are not to trust in formulas. Our trust is to be in the living God, who sees our needs and treats us as individuals.

God doesn't desire you to become introspective and guilt ridden through your mountain experiences. Instead, He desires for you to see His power and loving concern in these times.

In the book of the prophet Zechariah, we are given the account of how God handled a particular mountain facing one of His children. Zerubbabel was governor of Judah and he loved the

Lord. He was ruler over a people who had grown cold towards God. Their apathy was well expressed in the act of allowing the house of God to be in a state of disrepair while they each worked on their own homes. They just didn't care about God anymore, and Zerubbabel didn't know how to handle the problem. He was supposed to be their leader, and yet he was powerless in this situation. He could issue orders to his people, but he couldn't change their hearts. He was faced with a mountain.

Listen to what the Lord said to His child, "This is the word of the Lord to Zerubbabel saying, 'Not by might nor by power, but by My Spirit' says the Lord of hosts. 'What are you, O great mountain? Before Zerubbabel you will become a plain; and he will bring forth the top stone with shouts of "Grace, grace to it!" ' " (4:6&7).

There are a number of great truths to see in this account. First, God specifically told Zerubbabel the removal of this mountain would not, and could not, be accomplished through his own might or power. Second, Zerubbabel was told this was a matter which would be handled through the Spirit of God. Third, we see God had chosen to use this situation to reveal to Zerubbabel His awesome and mighty power. God was going to make that mountain a plain right in front of His child so Zerubbabel would witness an unforgetable demonstration of God's powerful love commitment to him.

You see, Zerubbabel was being told to have faith, but it wasn't the type of faith where the responsibility of victory was being made dependant upon his belief. The faith being spoken of here was simply a faith in God's concern. It was a faith in God taking responsibility for this mountain. Zerubbabel was able to rest in the Lord, because he was given a promise.

Now look closely at the last section of this verse, "And he will bring forth the top stone with shouts of 'Grace, grace to it'." This seems rather cryptic, doesn't it? Yet it's here in Scripture, and God obviously had a reason for saying this. Do you have any idea what the phrase, "top stone", refers to? Perhaps if I explain what it means in Hebrew it will become clearer to you. Eh-ben-ro-shaẃ is the Hebrew word for top stone and it literally means: "stone of the head." Who is the head? Who is our Cornerstone and Rock of our salvation? Jesus! This is our Lord being spoken of here. Keep in mind Zechariah lived long before Jesus ever came to earth. So here we have God telling Zerubbabel about Jesus taking care of his mountains. Isn't this fantastic?

What do you think Zerubbabel's reaction to a revelation of Jesus would be? God tells us in this verse. He says, "He will bring forth the top stone with shouts of 'Grace, grace to it'." Young's Literal Translation of the Bible puts the verse this way: "And he hath brought forth the top stone, cries of 'Grace, grace-are to it'." You see, Zerubbabel isn't shouting "Grace, grace" to the mountain. No. He is shouting "Grace, grace" to the top stone.

When you have a revelation of Christ, He becomes bigger than your mountains and, as a matter of fact, you stop seeing your mountains altogether as your eyes are fixed upon Him. When you see God remove your mountains, you are confronted with "Grace, grace."

God's grace removes mountains. Isn't this truth better than thinking it's somehow all up to you? Wouldn't you rather see Jesus and His grace, instead of beholding your mountain? You can, for this is God's way.

Understanding this, perhaps another verse will make sense to you. In the Gospel of Mark, Jesus said, "Truly I say to you, whoever says to this mountain 'Be taken up and cast into the sea,' and does not doubt in his heart, but believes that what he says is going to happen, it shall be granted him. Therefore I say to you, all things for which you pray and ask, believe that you have received them, and they shall be granted you" (Mark 11:23&24).

Contrary to what some would have you believe, this Scripture is not a blank check for you to go out and claim whatever you want. You have to take all of God's word, as I said earlier, and that means you have to consider this statement in the light of praying according to the will of God. "Thy will be done" is essential to a true understanding of what Jesus is communicating here.

Does this verse make sense to you now? Perhaps in the past you wondered how on earth you would be able to remove a mountain. Maybe you thought the faith being spoken of here was a type of power you work up within yourself. If you are willing to look at God's grace, and if you are willing to believe *He* will remove your mountains through His grace, then I tell you, having faith will be no problem for you at all. You will be free from thinking God requires you to remove your trials. You will become liberated into the true knowledge that God only asks you to believe in His ability and desire to handle your mountains for you.

Once you see your Stone of the Head, Jesus, you too will be shouting "Grace, grace", and you will forever know, regardless of whatever mountain confronts you, God will be there to make it a plain in front of your eyes so you will see a vivid display of His mighty and magnificent grace.

# Chapter 11

# The Establishment of Your Heart

*"Be not carried away with divers and strange doctrines. For it is a good thing that the heart be established with grace."*
**Hebrews 13:9 (King James)**

Where does your heart live? What I mean is, what is it your heart dwells most often upon? The answer to this question will tell you where your heart lives.

If you are overwhelmed with anger, that's where your heart lives. If unforgiveness is eating away at you, that's where your heart lives. If you are constantly thinking about your financial problems, then that's where your heart lives.

You may feel like stopping me and saying, "But Wayne, I'm a Christian. My heart lives in Jesus." I hope your heart does live in Jesus. However I have discovered there are many Christians who do confess Jesus as Lord, and yet have an incredibly difficult time seeing His truth become reality. In other words, when I speak about where your heart lives, I'm speaking in terms of actual experience, not in terms of theological declarations. If you have been born again, your heart truly is in Jesus, but I'm referring to the here and nowness of things.

The point is, whatever we allow to rule our thought life in experience, will determine where our heart is in experience.

Wouldn't you like to have your heart in a place where it wouldn't be carried away every time something went wrong? Wouldn't it be great to have your heart so that it wouldn't always be drifting away from Christ? Well, it is possible and as a matter of fact, God's Word declares to us that this is to be so for our lives.

Hebrews 13:9 says, "Be not carried away with divers and strange doctrines. For it is a good thing that the heart be established with grace" (King James version). Are you willing to believe that any doctrine which does not focus on grace is, in fact, a divers and strange doctrine? You may think this is carrying it a bit too far, but I really don't think so. It is so important to stay in the grace of God. Step out for only a moment and it's like leaving the calm eye of the hurricane to be swept into the whirling vortex of divers teachings. Remember, grace is 100% God. Most other teachings, which don't have their basis in grace, are partially God and partially you teachings. They are so easy to become deceived in, for as I said earlier, our old Adamic nature wants to get involved. Not involved with serving God, but involved with trying to usurp God's authority in our lives by deceiving us into walking by our own power. Do you suppose that's possible?

Let me try to explain this further. Adam, our old nature, hates God and never the two shall meet. God's growth and transforming power takes place in our new nature, which has been created in the likeness of God. Every day we walk in our new nature is a day in which Adam loses more and more ground, and he doesn't like that. He wants the spotlight. He wants to play center stage.

He's a crafty fellow, so, he says, "If you can't beat 'em, join 'em." He'll try to make you think you need his help in order to be a better Christian. He'll whisper noble thoughts into your heart like, "God can only use a holy vessel. So let's work hard at making you holy." If you are not rooted in grace, you just might listen to that thought, and off you go, trying to attain through your efforts what God has already granted, namely holiness.

It's not that Adam wants to serve God. He only wants to be on the throne of your life. But he is clever, and he will try to persuade you into thinking you need his help. He knows that if you try to earn God's blessings through your flesh, you will wind up in failure and once again completely under his domination. He'll be glad to give you a hand for awhile, but as in all things, you will surely reap what you sow.

Who is behind the Adamic nature? Satan, the great deceiver, the accuser of the brethren. Before we became born again we were of our father the devil (John 8:44). We walked and thought according to the Adamic nature because that's all we had, and the bottom line was that the Adamic nature was actually of Satan. The prince of darkness had manipulated our lives with ease because he had us duped into believing we were actually the captains of our own destinies.

This may sound extreme to you. If it does then I suggest you consider what you really were before Christ saved you.

Remember the fall of Lucifer. His separation from God came as the result of his desire to ascend to heaven and make himself as the Most High (Isaiah 14:12-14). He began thinking independently of God. He became the center of his own life and his selfish desires were made manifest as he took one third of the angels in heaven into his own dominion by feeding them the same lie that they could, and should, be as God (Revelation 12:3&4). They were cast down, defeated completely at the cross of Calvary (Hebrews 2:14, 1 John 3:8, Colossians 2:15) and now they themselves are possessed by their own evil.

In the garden, when Satan came as the serpent to Eve, he fed her and deceived her with the same lie, "You will be like God" (Genesis 3:5). Eve, followed by Adam, both ate of the same lie and were cast away from God's presence. Ever since that time, every soul born has been born into Adam's rebellion, so it is only "natural" for each one of us to have lived with this same independent and self serving nature (Romans 5:12).

We may think nothing of our former manner of life, but when we trace it back to its beginnings we see Satan as the one who instituted the system of independence from God. So, Jesus was not exaggerating in the least when He declared, "You are of your father the devil."

But you may say, "I'm born again, so what does this have to do with my heart in this day?" I've taken this brief side track to show you how deceived we can be when we try to live the Christian life by our own power.

Don't you see where this self centered thinking comes from? It's simply Satan, disguising himself as us, trying to draw us away from our utter dependency upon God.

The devil knows he has lost your soul to Christ, but his evil is total, so he will try to manipulate your "walk" in the Lord. If he can get you to swallow the lie that you need to help God, then he knows you will become focused upon yourself, outside of Christ, and he will once again be able to dominate your experiential life.

The truth is, you have been crucified with Christ. Your old Adamic nature died when you were born again. Nevertheless you live, but it's not you, not the old you. Now it is Christ who lives in you. He has become your life (Galatians 2:20).

I've heard this said many times, "If I am dead, why do I feel so alive?" The answer to that question is, as I have said, Satan will not give up even though he knows he has already lost. So, he tries to convince you that the old you is the real you. He wants you to live in a self consciousness. He will do all he can to keep you from coming into the reality of a Christ consciousness.

The Bible is true. You did die with Christ. Your old self is done with. You are a new creation (2nd Corinthians 5:17). You have been created in righteousness and holiness of the truth. The only thing you must do is lay aside the old self, the old independent and separated thinking. When you do that you will be able to put on your new self. This happens by the renewing of your mind (Ephesians 4:22-24). You must allow your thinking to be re-newed, changed from the old to the new.

You are not two people. There is not a good you and a bad you. It is true that the spirit and flesh wage war with each other as Galatians 5:17 says, but this does not mean there are two you's. Your real true self is in Christ. You are a spirit person. Those old holdovers from your former manner of life are not you anymore. You are hid with Christ in God (Colossians 3:3).

If you will walk in this truth, I tell you that you will see your-self become a whole person. You will at last be one with God. You will be free from feeling like a ping pong ball, always vacillating between the old and new natures. In the same way Christ's vic-tory swallowed up death (1st Corinthians 15:54), you will realize victory as you see your new nature swallow up the old. You will move from a Jekyll and Hyde perspective into a "To me, to live is Christ" knowing (Philippians 1:21).

Your real self emerges out of the cocoon as God's truth becomes your reality. Now, when some negative thought pops up, you can see it for what it really is, the devil trying to drag you away from your true identity. It's not you who thinks those things. That person died. Your real being is in Christ. Adam becomes unmasked. He is not you. He is the manifestation of Satan, attempting to persuade you away from God.

The only way these great truths will become resident in your heart will be as you allow your thoughts to be established in the grace of God. Grace is your effective bulwark against every strange and divers teaching. Grace keeps you in spirit truth. Grace protects you from the deceptive snares of the evil one. Grace is the essence of Jesus and is therefore the essence of the true you in Christ. This is why "it is good for the heart to be established with grace." Grace establishes your heart in one place, as a wholly integrated and complete person. Grace frees you from the split personality trap which so many Christians fall into.

If your heart lives in grace, then you're aware 100% of the time that only God can handle situations. Thus when your anger begins to rise, or when the financial outlook darkens, you know only God can take care of it. You realize He is the one with the power, and so you are spared from another fruitless attempt at trying to control your life through your own power, which as we saw is really Satan's power trying to take opportunity through the disguise of Adam.

Let your heart be established with grace today, Beb-ah-yŏ-o, is the Greek word used for established in this verse and its meaning is; to be stable and confirmed. Incidentally, this word comes from baś-ece, which is where our English words, basis and base, come from. If you are willing to live in God's grace, then the word here is that you will be stable and established. Doesn't this sound good?

It's time to come out from under the dominion of your old nature. You can, if you will let your heart be established with grace. You have suffered long enough. You have drifted in divers teachings long enough. Stay in grace. Grace will always point you to Jesus and in Him you will find your true life.

You need not be overwhelmed with anger, frustration, and guilt. These things are not the real you. You will *know* experiential victory in your life if you will only let your heart be established with grace.

# Chapter 12

# Grace Produces Obedience

*"We have received grace and apostleship to bring about the obedience of the faith among all the gentiles, for His name's sake."*                                    ***Romans 1:15***

The main argument usually raised against grace is this: "People who live only in grace will go off on their own and commit all kinds of horrible sins." This accusation is not valid, and it is based totally upon ignorance and supposition. The ignorance is obvious, for any person who says such a thing regarding grace simply does not understand what grace is, and the supposition is that grace is only one part of God's plan for us, the part which saves us, while the law must be God's plan to keep us in line. Hopefully, at this point, I trust statements such as these will seem like sheer nonsense to you. We know grace is Jesus, and we know the law is only powerful in terms of revealing sin, not in keeping us from it.

Those who say these things may be well intentioned, however

good intentions don't count for much when you are wrong. At the end of this age, when some soul appears before Jesus and says, "But I tried to do good all my life", that won't be able to save him. His intention doesn't save him. Salvation is determined solely by what that person did with Jesus. Suppose he says, "No, I couldn't believe Jesus really died for my sins, so I thought I'd try to save myself." Will he be saved? No, because at that point he has rejected the Lord and has instead made God in his own image.

Christians who reject God's grace for their ongoing walk and instead adopt some works maintenance program may be well intentioned, but nevertheless, they are wrong. Some person may self-righteously pat himself on the back and say, "I keep all my church ordinances and laws" and he may believe he is the epitome of obedience. But, that's not obedience. True obedience is seeing what God's word declares and then obeying it. If God's word says the law brings about wrath and that the Christian is to live in grace, then to live in the law is disobedience.

You see, people today have drawn the erronious conclusion that obedience is synonymous with works. This is not obedience. Obedience is obeying the word of God. If God's word says rest, then the only way you will obey that word is for you to rest. This is hard to communicate.

When we first come to Christ and are saved, we are so in love with and thankful to our glorious Lord. We know He saved us and we couldn't save ourselves. But, very often here is where we allow the mistake to come in. While we should be feasting upon our Bread of Life, Jesus, and being filled with the knowledge of what His finished work means for our lives, we instead embark upon a path of trying to please God. This is a "natural" outcome, and I emphasize the word natural. Our desire, while being well intentioned, is born out of the mistaken concept that we need to pay God for what He has given us. The result is we immediately cut ourselves off completely from the knowledge of who Jesus is, and we run headlong into a service oriented lifestyle.

I'm all for good works, but I think it is tragic when a Christian falls so rapidly from grace back into the world's way of thinking. You know the old "You pay for what you get" mentality. If there is one thing we need desperately to see in our new birth, it's the true character and nature of God. But in our zeal, I'm afraid we many times are guilty of running into service before we have received our marching orders.

Christians who have spent years in that type of sad state have almost developed a hatred for grace. They look to themselves and are deluded into thinking they are keeping themselves holy, so they certainly don't want to hear of any system of holiness by grace. If they worked for theirs, you can be sure they want you to work for yours too. It is so sad, because the works system is full of fear. If you fall down, you're out, under that way of living. You can try to obey all your life, but lose your temper and then get hit be a car and, in that system, you will wind up in hell. You see, their Jesus has no power or covering protection. At best, He is a cheerleader on the sidelines urging you on. Works depend upon you, and that is why there is so much fear and misery in that theology. This is why teaching upon grace is such an offense to a legalist's ears.

Let me share this verse of Scripture with you, "We have received grace and apostleship to bring about the obedience of the faith among all the gentiles, for His name's sake" (Romans 1:5). According to this verse, it is grace which brings about obedience. Apostleship represents the office and authority God had given

Paul to minister, and grace is the power under which Paul would minister. Grace brings about obedience!

This statement from the Bible is in direct opposition to statements made by those who would paint grace as some license to sin. As we saw in an earlier chapter, grace is the only *true* freedom from sin. So in this setting, to receive grace is to be obedient. If God says grace produces obedience, then to say anything else produces obedience is actually being disobedient.

What an absolute delight to realize that the grace of our Lord Jesus filling our hearts keeps us in His will. I can't think of a better way to walk in the Lord than that. What a relief to see works is not the way to maintain salvation, but that God is in us and He does the maintaining. What glorious rest! In an atmosphere permeated with the love of God such as this, you will find yourself springing forth in good works. Not good works to earn something from God, or prove something to Him, but good works which are the result of a heart realization of the grace in Jesus which saves us, keeps us, fills us, sustains us, and blesses us. This knowledge of grace does indeed bring about the obedience of the faith.

# Chapter 13

# Grace Produces Fruit

*"We give thanks to God, the Father of our Lord Jesus Christ, praying always for you, since we heard of your faith in Christ Jesus and the love which you have for all the saints; because of the hope laid up for you in heaven, of which you previously heard in the word of truth, the Gospel, which has come to you, just as in all the world also it is constantly bearing fruit and increasing, even as it has been doing in you also since the day you heard of it and understood the grace of God in truth."* **Colossians 1:3-6**

In the last chapter we saw the truth of grace producing our obedience. Now we will go one more step and see it is grace which produces our fruit.

Jesus said, "You did not choose Me, but I chose you, and appointed you, that you should go and bear fruit, and that your fruit should remain" (John 15:16). First and foremost, we must see when it comes to bearing fruit, it is not a case of our striving according to the power of the flesh. Our fruit bearing process begins with Jesus. "You did not choose Me, but I chose you." That's the Scripture given to us. In other words, our life began with God, and not with us. He chose us before we chose Him, and that's the way He wants our life to continue. Any decision we make should be based first upon the decision He has made. If we decide to preach the word of God to a gathering today, our decision should be made only if His Spirit has already decided this for us. "Thy will be done, and not my will" is to be our heart cry.

Second, once we have this truth straight in our hearts, we can then see that the subject of bearing fruit has also been created and decided by Him. "And appointed you, that you should go and bear fruit." Suppose you went downtown today, stood on the street corner, and then declared to all there that they had to vacate the city within one hour. Would they do it? No, they wouldn't. You would be laughed at. But suppose you said you had been appointed by the president to make this declaration, and suppose you showed in writing your appointment. Then the result would be different, wouldn't it? What is it that would make the difference? Your appointment. If you haven't been appointed then you don't have any power or authority. But if you have been appointed, then you do have the necessary power to get the job done.

You have been appointed, and you have the power. Jesus has appointed you to go and bear fruit. If you don't realize God has willed it for you to bear fruit, then I'm afraid you will probably wind up in a frustrated state of mind, feeling that bearing fruit is something you perform. You will be just like the person trying to deliver the message without any appointment. You'll try, but nothing will happen. However, if you understand it is God who has made this decision, then you will realize, "Faithful is He who calls you, and He also will bring it to pass" (1st Thessalonians 5:24). You will know you can rest and trust in His word. This is bearing fruit according to grace.

I've spoken with many Christians who feel their lives are worthless because they don't see any fruit. They have become guilt ridden and introspective because they figure there must be something wrong with them. Or, they have begun to feel perhaps God doesn't love them as much as He loves His other children. This is not true! God is no respector of persons. He loves us all equally and totally.

The worst thing we can do to ourselves, when things begin to go wrong, is to follow our feelings instead of God's Word. Our feelings draw us inside ourselves and we start focusing upon all our rather obvious faults. We conclude this must be why God isn't using us. On the other hand, God's Word draws us away from ourselves and into the full provision of Jesus Christ for our lives. God's Word reveals that grace is the basis of His operation in our lives, and it is not a matter of some self perfection. God's Word shows us He produces our fruit. The problem, in most cases, is that those whom I have spoken to were trying to do God's job. They were laboring under the illusion that fruit is produced simply by their own works, and no fruit would appear, because they never gave the Lord a chance.

God produces fruit in our lives via His grace. Paul wrote, in his first letter to the Corinthian church, "I planted, Apollos watered, but God was causing the growth. So then neither the one who plants nor the one who waters is anything, but God who causes the growth" (3:6&7). We need to remember at all times it is God who causes the growth.

God has taken the responsibility for your growth. If you are willing to believe this, then you will really start to bear fruit. You can't speed up God's process of growth in your life, but you sure can slow it down if you try to do His job. Let God be God. Understand what His word says and you will bear fruit.

The first chapter of Colossians says, "We give thanks to God, the Father of our Lord Jesus Christ, praying always for you, since we heard of your faith in Christ Jesus and the love which you have for all the saints; because of the hope laid up for you in heaven, of which you previously heard in the word of truth, the Gospel, which has come to you, just as in all the world also it is constantly bearing fruit and increasing, even as it has been doing in you also since the day youy heard of it and understood the grace of God in truth" (1:3-6).

I would like you to pay close attention to the last part of this Scripture. According to these verses, how did the Gospel bear fruit and increase in the Colossian believers? Was it by their efforts? No, it was by hearing and understanding the grace of God in truth. God's grace is the active ingredient in the fruit bearing process. It's grace which makes our fruit spring forth.

Two things are said concerning grace in this portion of Scripture. First, you must hear it. You have got to be willing to listen to the word of God's grace. Second, you must understand it. The word you hear must have real meaning to you.

I suppose it would be possible for someone to read this entire book, and still have no idea what God's grace is. If you think because you read something then that means you understand what you read, you are wrong. You have to meditate upon what you read. You have to ask God to make it real to you. Don't settle for just an intellectual grasp of things. Don't content yourself with simply reading something. The Bible says you must hear and understand.

This word from Colossians promises you and I that the word of truth, the Gospel, will increase and bear fruit in us if we will hear and understand the grace of God in truth.

Look at it this way. We know God causes our growth, right? Then this must mean we are like a plant. So, in this framework, look upon God's grace as the rich soil in which you are planted. As you stay in grace, God, our Gardener, will have the maximum opportunity to cause us to grow and bear fruit. Not only will we achieve our full potential in Christ, but we will also have the great privilege and blessing of being surrounded and protected by the magnificent grace of our Lord Jesus.

"Today if you hear His voice, do not harden your hearts" (Hebrews 4:7). Hear the word of grace, and ask our Lord to grant you a heart of understanding. As you dwell in your spirit upon the grace in Jesus, He will cause fruit to come forth, and your fruit will remain. Remember, He is the vine and we are the branches. Let the life of the vine flow through you today.

# Chapter 14

# Real Growth is in Grace

*"And now I commend you to God and to the word of His grace, which is able to build you up and to give you the inheritance among all those who are sanctified."*                    *Acts 20:32*

*"Grow in the grace and knowledge of our Lord and Savior Jesus Christ. To Him be the glory, both now and to the day of eternity. Amen."*                    *2nd Peter 3:18*

Paul and Barnabas had set out on their first missionary journey together. After preaching the word in Paphos, they went on into the regions of Galatia. After arriving in Pisidian Antioch, on the sabbath day they went into the synagogue. When the reading of the law and the prophets was finished, Paul was asked if he had anything to say. He stood up and began to speak of our risen Lord and Savior Jesus Christ. At the close of the service this is what happened: "And as Paul and Barnabas were going out, the people kept begging that these things might be spoken to them the next sabbath. Now when the meeting of the synagogue had broken up, many of the Jews and of the God-fearing proselytes followed Paul and Barnabas, who, speaking to them, were urging them to continue in the grace of God" (Acts 13:42&43).

What was it Paul and Barnabas admonished the people to do? Continue in the grace of God. Today many people are willing to accept grace for salvation, but they are not willing to continue in the grace of God. Paul preached grace for salvation, and he also preached grace for growth.

The simplest way of saying it is; the grace that saves you will also keep, grow, and perfect you. If you want to stay on track with God, then continue in His grace. If you want to realize all your spiritual blessings, then continue in grace. If you want to see God's promises become reality, then continue in His grace. Grace is the key to real Christian growth.

How sad and tragic it is when many Christians pass up the grace of God because they believe there are "deeper things" for them to learn. When you really think about it, this type of pseudo-spiritual quest for deeper things is a charade. Wouldn't you say that Jesus is the deepest of all truths? Well, then what makes you think you will unlock the door to victorious life in anything other than Jesus? In reality, those who leave behind grace in order to see the so called deep things are only expressing their spiritual immaturity.

To say, "I've got Jesus, let's see what else I can get," and then to go searching after all the current winds of doctrine, is to do precisely the most detremental thing you can do to your growth process. God will let you chase these tangents for as long as you want but, praise His name, He'll also be waiting with open arms to re-establish you in His grace when you are weary and realize these side tracks are nothing but dead ends.

If you make up your mind to continue in the grace of God, you will insure your well being in Jesus Christ.

Later on in His ministry, Paul was being compelled by the Holy Spirit to go to Jerusalem, even though he knew bonds and imprisonment awaited him. On Paul's way there, his ship stopped at Miletus and he called for the elders of the Ephesian church to meet him. He knew this was the last time he would ever see these spiritual children of his. As Paul closed his address to them he said, "Therefore be on the alert, remembering that night and day for a period of three years I did not cease to admonish each one with tears. And now I commend you to God and to the word of His grace, which is able to build you up and to give you the inheritance among all those who are sanctified" (Acts 20:31&32).

Paul's message was still the same! Perhaps you wondered as he grew if Paul's emphasis had been altered at all. Maybe the Lord had revealed some better and deeper way to him. No, God's plan of salvation and growth remained unchanged, and Paul's message remained unchanged, because he cared first and foremost for ministering the word of God in truth and accuracy.

He commended his beloved brethren and children in the faith to God's grace. In other words, he entrusted them to grace for he knew grace would take care of them. He knew grace would protect them and he knew grace would reveal to them true growth and maturity.

He said grace would build them up. If there was any spiritual construction to be done in their lives, Paul knew only grace could do it. He also said grace would give them their inheritance. It's not that they didn't have an inheritance, for they did. What Paul was expressing here was that grace was the only way for them to realize what was already theirs in Jesus Christ.

May we understand these truths in our hearts. May we commend ourselves fully to the grace of God. As I mentioned in the last chapter, grace is the soil in which we can grow. Grace is the climate which will keep us in the peak of spiritual health. As we continue in the grace of God, we will be experientially walking in the realization of the greatest love the world has ever known.

There is one more verse I would like to share with you concerning growing in grace. As his life neared its end, Peter committed some final thoughts to print. It was as if he were summing up his whole relationship with God in a few concise words so that those who would believe after him would have the benefit of his life in the Lord. At the close of his last letter Peter said, "Grow in the grace and knowledge of our Lord and Savior Jesus Christ. To Him be the glory, both now and to the day of eternity. Amen" (2nd Peter 3:18).

Peter knew that even if you were to forget everything else, if you would just keep your heart in the grace and knowledge of Jesus Christ, then you would grow in all of God's fullness.

So many of the so called deeper life teachings don't even mention Jesus Christ, let alone revolve around Him. This should set off a warning signal in your spirit whenever you hear such things being taught. What's really important is to stay Christ centered, and the only way to remain in a Christ centered relationship, where Jesus truly is in the center, is to remain in the grace of God.

Today you have an opportunity to grow in the grace and knowledge of our Lord and Savior Jesus Christ. Look at His true nature. See what He has accomplished for you. See who you are in Him. Focusing your attention upon these things will lead you directly into the grace of God every time. God's grace will build you up, if you are willing to continue in it. God's grace will bring you a revelation of Jesus in your own life, if you are willing to seek your growth through His grace. Live in His grace right now and you will find He will do in you exceedingly abundantly beyond all you could ever ask or think.

# Chapter 15

# Grace and Hope

*" . . . Our Lord Jesus Christ Himself and God our Father, who has loved us and given us eternal comfort and good hope by grace . . . "*             *2nd Thessalonians 2:16*

*"Fix your hope completely on the grace to be brought to you at the revelation of Jesus Christ."*         *1st Peter 1:13*

As Paul closed the thirteenth chapter of his first letter to the Corinthian church, concluding his moving message on the paramount importance of love, he said, "But now abide faith, hope, and love, these three; but the greatest of these is love" (verse 13).

We have seen in this book that God's expression of love to the world is through Jesus Christ. His life, death, and resurrection all came about as a result of His love for us. When His love became flesh, grace appeared to us all. Love is the heart of God towards us, and grace is that love made manifest. Love is the greatest, for all things are held together and have been accomplished through the love of God.

What I would like to look at in this chapter is the word, hope. We hear a lot of people speaking of faith these days, and we hopefully hear a lot about God's love, but hope seems to be the least spoken of. Yet the Bible says, faith, hope, and love are the three abiding elements. Why is it so many different things are being expounded upon, when we see right here that faith, hope, and love is where our attention should be?

Perhaps people don't know what to hope in. Maybe that's why we hear so little about this important word.

What do we need to hope for? We have a complete salvation in Jesus Christ, so we don't need to hope for what we already have. We have the Holy Spirit living inside us, so we need not hope for His presence. As a matter of fact, you may think that any Christian who knows the promises of God would not hope at all, for he should realize and accept those promises.

Yet the Bible says hope remains.

What we need to do at this point, is to look at what we think hope means, and what the Bible says hope means.

When a person says he hopes something will happen, what he usually means is he wants to see that thing come to pass, but he is not sure it will.

To us, hope means the desire for something, but without a complete confidence of it happening. There is always an element of uncertainty when we speak of hope.

According to the Bible, hope means something quite different. The Greek word for hope in the New Testament is ĕlpis, which means, to anticipate with pleasure, or to have expectation and confidence.

Are you in some trial right now? Is there a big Goliath in your path threatening to grind you into the dust? Has some family or financial trouble left you weak and exhausted? If you are in any difficulty at all, the good news here is to hope in the Lord. Not an "I'm not sure" hope, or an "I'd like to have hope but I'm not good enough" type of hope either, but a "confident anticipation with pleasure" hope. That's the type of hope the Scriptures speak of.

When the Bible speaks of hope, there is no room for uncertainty. There is only a complete assurance, an eager looking forward. This may trouble you at first. You may be thinking to yourself that this is the type of hope you want, but just can't quite get. If that is what you're thinking, then you must be putting the burden of hope upon yourself.

Hope is not a positive mind-set to psych yourself into. Hope is something God produces in us. It is His job to give us hope.

Would you like to see your hope transformed from one with uncertainty to one with an expectation and confidence; an anticipation with pleasure? Look carefully at this next verse, and let the full meaning sink into your spirit. ". . . Our Lord Jesus Christ Himself and God our Father, who has loved us and given us eternal comfort and good hope by grace . . ." (2nd Thessalonians 2:16). How can we have this good hope? The answer to this question is the same as the answer to so many other questions we have looked at in this book; God's grace.

You see, when we get into a difficult situation we tend to become introspective and totally problem conscious. In that frame of mind, we often assume it's up to us to try and work things out but we will never solve anything by relying upon our own strength or ability.

Many of you know that. You don't look for an answer from within yourself. You are looking to the Lord. You hope in Him.

But there is still that uncertainty in your hope. Even though we say we are looking to the Lord, sometime the truth is we are not looking at His grace. Without grace there is uncertainty, because you may wonder if God really cares enough to deliver you. You may wonder if He is holding back His hand of power due to some fault or shortcoming He has noticed in you. When you say you are looking to the Lord, but you aren't looking at His grace, then you really are not looking to the Lord. What you are doing is looking at your trial and hoping with uncertainty that God will see your trial too.

When you truly look to God, you will see His grace, and hope will be born in your heart. Grace will give you the hope, the vision you need. Grace will bring you out of the narrow realm of time and space tribulation into the vast storehouse of God's riches. Grace gives you a "good hope", as the Bible says. Grace points you to Jesus Christ, and to His complete, committed, and unconditional love for you. Grace says, "I will never leave you nor forsake you" (Hebrews 13:5). Instead of hoping without confidence, you will know grace is God's sure word of deliverance to you, and you will anticipate with pleasure. The answer God is bringing will become more real to you than the trial itself, and you will rejoice! You will have confidence! You will be expecting the answer any moment because you have seen grace, and grace gives you hope! Grace is hope purified.

Can you see the important role hope is to play in our life? Now abide faith, hope, and love. We hope because God's promise is greater than any tribulation. Whether it be the world, the flesh, or the devil, it doesn't matter, because we have seen grace. God's grace saved us, justified us, redeemed us, and God's grace plants hope in our heart.

Whenever you get down, lift up your head, behold the grace of God, and you will be transformed into His image.

There is one more verse I would like to share with you. This is an exhortation and I believe you will be able to recognize its importance now. "Fix your hope completely on the grace to be brought to you at the revelation of Jesus Christ" (1st Peter 1:13).

Our hope is to be completely, 100%, fixed upon grace. When we place our hope upon God's grace, then our hope becomes real Bible hope, that anticipation with pleasure. If you hope in anything other than grace, then you will only be insuring the return of uncertainty to your life.

At first glance you may only consider this verse as a reference to the second coming of Jesus. But look at it more carefully. Think of it in terms of having meaning for your life right now. What is it saying? Real hope means you are looking to Jesus, and when you have a revelation of Him, as He is, grace will be brought to you, because that is what His true essence is. Fix your hope completely on the grace to be brought to you at the revelation of Jesus Christ.

Hope means more than looking to the Lord. Real hope means you know what God is like. You have that confidence and expectation because you know your hope in the Lord is hope in His grace which will never let you down.

How would you like to have a revelation of Jesus today? Receive His grace, walk in it, live in it, and base your life upon it. Do this and Jesus will be revealed to you because grace is His heart. Once you know Jesus in this way, you will find hope to be a very powerful and relevant force in your life, for hope means you know God's grace will always bring you triumphantly through all things, no matter how great or small. Grace produces steadfast hope, and hope enables you to see the hand of God for you in your darkest moment.

Praise God for the wonderful blessing of hope. It's a good hope He gives to us.

# Chapter 16

# The Throne of Grace

*"We do not have a high priest who cannot sympathize with our weaknesses, but one who has been tempted in all things as we are, yet without sin. Let us therefore draw near with confidence to the throne of grace, that we may receive mercy and may find grace to help in time of need."*     *Hebrews 4:15&16*

Have you ever noticed our tendency in human nature to look down upon someone who has a weakness we do not have? Unfortunately, this trait runs rampant and is even encouraged in Christian circles. You don't have to search too far in order to hear a message which comes across in a "holier than thou" fashion. How many people, who need Jesus, have been turned off to the Gospel, not because they have hardened their hearts, but because the only Christianity they have been exposed to has been the "you filthy sinner" presentation so many preachers think God wants them to deliver? A man would certainly be hard pressed to find even one Scripture where Jesus ever ministered in that way. Yet this type of message goes on, mainly because it appeals to man's ego. There is something dark in the old heart of each of us which loves to be compared to others, as long as we come out on top.

Isn't it true, that in order for anyone to look down upon another, they must be personally taking the credit for where they are? The Christian who has been delivered from a life of sin and death, and then goes about criticizing and judging others around him who are still in that state, truly does not know the full revelation of God's forgiveness and he doesn't understand the desperate condition he was once in. The believer who has had a battle with some fault, is set free from it by the Lord, and then harshly comes down upon a brother or sister undergoing the same problem, is obviously ignorant of the grace of God and is in fact saying, "I'm better than you, because I don't do that thing anymore." Such attitudes are foreign to the Word of God and yet are found nowhere more abundantly than in the church today. How can this be?

There is an incident recorded in the Gospel of Luke which strikes at the heart of this issue. Jesus had been invited to dinner at a Pharisee's house, and while they were reclining at table, a woman entered and coming to Jesus, began wiping His feet with her hair and tears. The Pharisee thought to himself, "If this man were a prophet He would know who and what sort of person this woman is who is touching Him, that she is a sinner" (7:39). Jesus perceived his thoughts and said in reply to him, "A certain money lender had two debters: one owed five hundred denari, and the other fifty. When they were unable to repay, he graciously forgave them both. Which of them therefore will love him more?" Simon (the Pharisee) answered and said, "I suppose the one whom he forgave more." And He said to him, "You have judged correctly." And turning toward the woman, He said to Simon, "Do you see this woman? I entered your house; you gave Me no water for My feet, (a common custom of the day) but she has wet

My feet with her tears, and wiped them with her hair. You gave Me no kiss; but she, since the time I came in, has not ceased to kiss My feet. You did not anoint My head with oil, but she anointed My feet with perfume. For this reason I say to you, her sins, which are many, have been forgiven, for she loved much; but he who is forgiven little, loves little" (verses 41-47).

The Pharisee whom Jesus was dining with looked down upon this woman. He figured he was better than her because his outward conduct and external obedience to God was, in his own eyes, superior to her lifestyle. He was also judging Jesus as well for allowing this "sinner" to touch Him. In short, according to his standard of comparison, the law, he thought he was the closest of the three to God and he felt this entitled him to act in a haughty manner.

What is the point Jesus made in this situation? The great Spiritual truth manifest here is that the more you realize the forgiveness God has granted you, the more you will love Him in return. He who is forgiven much loves much, and he who is forgiven little loves little. In other words, the Christian who goes about rendering his opinion on every matter and person; criticizing, judging, and putting down, is only proclaiming to everyone that he thinks very little of the Lord's forgiveness for him. All he is doing is telling the world that when it comes to an understanding of God's gracious pardon, he knows nothing of it.

So, here is the church in this day and age, preaching salvation in Jesus Christ, and in some cases, living as if it doesn't know a thing about it. Anytime I hear a fire and brimstone "You dirty sinner" type of sermon, I cringe. My spirit is grieved, because I know how far that message is from the life and Gospel of my Lord.

It's not spiritual to look down on others. There is nothing admirable about saying "Well, I won't have anything to do with that person because he is into this sin or that sin." We have gotten this phony idea of holiness stuck in our heads. We think walking holy means steering clear of every sinner within one hundred miles. That's not holiness. All that is is running away from the very people God wants you to show His love to.

Actually, if you really want to know what the Bible says, take a look at this verse, "If a man is caught in any trespass, you who are spiritual, restore such a one in a spirit of gentleness; looking to yourselves, lest you too be tempted" (Galatians 6:1). As I have often taught, holiness is not the absence of sin in your life; holiness is the presence of Jesus. A truly spiritual person is not someone who thinks he has single handedly conquered every known sin in his life. Rather, he is someone who has received and experienced God's forgiveness and knows the presence of Jesus in his life. You declare to the world you know Jesus' presence in your life when you respond to a need, or fault, in the same way He does, with grace. This verse says here that the particular sin doesn't matter. "If a man is caught in *any* trespass." It's not the sin that matters here. What matters is your reaction to that sin and, according to the Bible, we are to react with a gentle spirit of restoration, remembering that we have the same tendencies and weaknesses as does anyone.

Chances are, the callous hard hearted judgmental Christian, would honestly feel he could never fall into that sin. He is a person who has not experientially met with the cross of Christ. There is still so much reliance upon his own ability or faith. He has not been broken to realize that without Christ he is nothing.

On the other hand, the truly spiritual person knows full well that all he is and has comes purely from the grace of God, so he will immediately respond to a situation like this with meekness and gentleness. His heart will go out to the one in sin. He will mourn over his condition. He will want to see that one restored. He will reach out his hand, remembering the time when Jesus stretched forth His hand when he was lost and living in a dead world. He will also bear in mind that, but for the grace of God, there he would be too.

Oh, how we need to see this! Thank God that He doesn't look down on us. Praise His name, He doesn't run from our sin. On the contrary, when you really think about it, what God actually did was to run into our sin. He saw our helpless condition and came to the rescue. Why? The only possible answer is because His love for us was greater than the sin we were in. The Bible says, "He made Him who knew no sin to be sin on our behalf, that we might become the righteousness of God in Him" (2nd Corinthians 5:21). He not only restored us, but in the process, He became the very sin we were lost in. He transferred it all from us on to Himself and at Calvary He received the full punishment due for our sin, death.

Certainly, if anyone had the right to exhibit a "holier than thou" attitude, Jesus did. He was the only one to ever live a full life and never once sin. Not once did he fall down. And not only that, but at the cross, as He hung there dying, He took all our sin upon Himself. Yes, if anyone had the right to put down, or criticize, He did. But, thankfully, He did not and does not look at us with a "holier than thou" attitude. If He did, where would we be?

Can you imagine falling into some sin, and then coming to God for assistance, if He was projecting an air of, "I'm better than you because I didn't do that"? Wouldn't you be afraid to come to the Lord if you thought that was the way He looked at you?

In fact, in my counselling ministry, I've talked to hundreds of Christians who are afraid to return to God, because they do think this is how God sees them. Invariably, they picked up this mistaken concept because that is how they were treated by their own brothers and sisters in Christ.

What is God's attitude? What ground do we stand on when we have fallen down? Are we going to receive some "spiritual chewing out"? Are we going to be cast into some second class Christian category? Or, worse yet, are we going to be thrown out of the family of God altogether?

No! Thank God the answer is no. I want you to look carefully at this extremely important passage of Scripture. Read it with thankfulness, and read it with reverence. "We do not have a high priest who cannot sympathize with our weaknesses, but one who has been tempted in all things as we are, yet without sin. Let us therefore draw near with confidence to the *throne of grace,* that we may receive mercy and may find grace to help in time of need" (Hebrews 4:15&16).

The magnificent truth is, Jesus never did fall into sin, but rather than put us down for our sin, He sympathizes with us. Because He is holy, He is free from all the comparison games we play and He sees us with love and compassion. When we realize this, we can, as the writer says, draw near with confidence.

You know, God could make His throne anything He wanted to. For instance, He could make His throne one of judgment if He desired. What could we say if that was what He chose? Nothing, for He is God and can do what He likes. He could make His throne one of condemnation, or criticism, or punishment, but He didn't. Instead, because He loves us, He chose to make His throne one of grace.

In ancient culture, the king would sit and rule over his people from his throne. If you had a dispute or problem, you would petition to see the king. If your petition was granted, you would enter that throne room with fear and trembling because you would not know the disposition of the king. He could rule in your favor and bless you, or he could rule against you and curse you.

We are not in that position because our King of Kings and Lord of Lords has proclaimed to us that His throne is one of grace. We know our King's disposition. That's why we can enter boldly. We can have confidence for He has already declared we will receive mercy and grace to help in time of need. God doesn't want to put us down. He wants to lift us up. God's throne is a throne of grace.

The Young's Literal Translation of the Bible reads this way, "We may come near, then, with freedom, to the throne of grace, that we may receive kindness, and find grace — for seasonable help." Can you imagine that you have the freedom, the unlimited access, given you by God Himself, to enter His throne room at any time? Whenever you do enter, the outcome will always be the same. You will be granted mercy, kindness, and grace.

God's help is seasonable. No matter what trial or difficulty you're in, God's help is there with you. He knows your hardship. He sees your weaknesses, and He sympathizes. He helps.

Christians, unaware of God's forgiveness, may continue their un-Christ like habits of comparison and putdown. But isn't it a relief to know God doesn't act like that? Isn't it good to know our Lord has a throne of grace where we can come whenever we have need and we will always receive His mercy? His grace will always be there for our time of need. I thank God that His spirituality is full of grace and forgiveness. I thank Him for establishing

His throne on grace and for throwing the doors wide open so we may enter at any time and be touched by our King.

# Chapter 17

# Grace Saves us
# From Death

*"But we do see Him who has been made for a little while lower than the angels, namely, Jesus, because of the suffering of death crowned with glory and honor, that by the grace of God He might taste death for everyone."*　　　　　***Hebrews 2:9***

In an earlier chapter we saw we are saved by the grace of God. We receive forgiveness for all our sins because of His wonderful grace. In this chapter, I would like you to think more about this. In particular, I would like you to think about how God's grace saves us from death.

This is something seldom spoken of, but it is just as great a blessing as the forgiveness of our sins. What do I mean when I say grace saves us from death? You may be wondering if I'm going to introduce some strange new doctrine. No, I'm not, but I do want to share with you that there is something very awesome which we have been saved from.

First, I should explain that I don't mean we won't ever die, in the sense of our physical bodies giving up. Unless the Lord returns first, you and I will reach the day when our flesh will be no more. But is this death? According to the world's definition it is, but according to God's definition it is not. Well then, what is God's definition of death?

In the 8th chapter of John's Gospel, Jesus said, "Truly, truly, I say to you, if anyone keeps My word he shall never see death" (verse 51). Is Jesus speaking of our bodies living forever? Are we dealing with the immortality of our flesh? No, that's not what He is saying, but He did say we should not see death. If you feel perplexed by His statement, you're not alone, because in the next verse the Jews replied, "Now we know that you have a demon. Abraham died, and the prophets also; and you say, 'If anyone keeps My word, he shall never taste of death' " (verse 52).

How are we to reconcile what Jesus said with the fact that our bodies die? In order to answer this question, we must look into what God considers death to be. Obviously, death in His eyes is more than the ceasing of life in our bodies.

Let's really think about this. We know heaven and earth will pass away someday, but we who know the Lord will live forever in eternal life. There is something alive in us, because of Jesus Christ, which will never die, and that something is our spirit. When the time arrives for our so called mortal coil to end its existence, what will happen to us? Do we cease to exist? No, on the contrary, that day will be the glorious moment when, as Paul writes, "What is mortal may be swallowed up by life" (2nd Corinthians 5:4). That day will be our liberation day! We will depart from the narrow confines of our physical limitations and enter into our glorious resurrection bodies. Those who were blind will see. Those who were lame will walk. Those who had suffered in this life with any physical or mental impediments will throw off their shackles and will run, dance, and sing as they are clothed with their new forms.

So, it's not accurate to say that a Christian dies, for this is not death. This is freedom and glory. This moment won't end anything for us, except our lives spent in this three dimensional sphere called time and space. You could hardly call this moment death.

Paul looked forward to this day. He had suffered much as he served the Lord. Affliction and adversity had been his constant companions as he traveled the known world, speaking of the resurrected One. In his letter to the Philippian church, he wrote, "For to me, to live is Christ, and to die is gain. But if I am to live on in the flesh, this will mean fruitful labor for me; and I do not know which to choose. But I am hard-pressed from both directions, having the desire to depart and be with Christ, for that is very much better; yet to remain on in the flesh is more necessary for your sake. And convinced of this, I know that I shall remain and continue with you all for your progress and joy in the faith" (1:21-25).

As much as Paul longed for the day when he would leave this world for the glory of seeing Christ face to face, he also knew God had a purpose for him in this sphere, namely, bringing others to a knowledge of the Savior, so they too might be delivered from death.

You can see, from what Scripture says, that instead of referring to ceasing of our natural life as death, we should be seeing this moment as our entrance into a final realization of the life which is our inheritance as children of the Lord. This is not death. This is life evermore. So, it is as Jesus said, we won't see death.

Then, what is death? If it is not when our bodies give up, then what is it?

In the book of Hebrews, chapter 2, the author says, "But we do see Him who has been made for a little while lower than the angels, namely, Jesus, because of the suffering of death crowned with glory and honor, that by the grace of God He might taste death for everyone" (verse 9). Jesus tasted death for us. He died, so we would not have to. He suffered for us, by His grace, so we would be free from that awful experience.

Do you know what was different about the death Jesus died? Do you know what sets His death apart from what you or I will ever experience?

When you yield your body, where will you go? The Bible tells us, "To be absent from the body and to be at home with the Lord" (2nd Corinthians 5:9). You and I will immediately be with the Lord in glory. As we have seen, this will be our graduation day.

When Jesus died, where did He go? Did He go to heaven for three days? No. Chapter 1 of Revelation says, "I am the first and the last, and the living one; and I was dead, and behold, I am alive forever more, and I have the keys of death and hades" (1:17&18). Jesus did not go to heaven. He went to hell! And that is real death, to leave your body and go to the domain of the evil one. As Revelation tells us, He went with a purpose. He seized the keys of death and hades from the devil and on the third day He rose again, to life forever. When we receive Jesus into our hearts as our Lord and Savior, His death becomes our death. We are gloriously freed from ever having to go through death. Jesus made it possible for you and I to be with Him in glory.

By the grace of God, He tasted death for everyone. The Greek word used for taste in this verse is gĕnŏmai, which means, to taste and experience. Jesus experienced death on our behalf so we would be spared this awful penalty, which we in fact deserved to receive. "The wages of sin is death, but the free gift of God is eternal life in Christ Jesus our Lord" (Romans 6:23). Without Jesus we would surely have died, in the biblical sense. We would have spent eternity apart from God in the lake of fire (see Revelation 20:15). But now, because of our Savior, we will never taste death, for He tasted it on our behalf.

As far as God is concerned, we will never die! "This perishable must put on the imperishable, and this mortal must put on immortality. But when this perishable will have put on the imperishable, and this mortal will have put on immortality, then will come about the saying that is written 'DEATH IS SWALLOWED UP IN VICTORY. O DEATH, WHERE IS YOUR VICTORY? O DEATH, WHERE IS YOUR STING?' The sting of death is sin, and the power of sin is the law; but thanks be to God, who gives us the victory through our Lord Jesus Christ" (1st Corinthians 15:53-57).

By the grace of God, we have been saved from death. We are free! Think about this. If you know Jesus Christ, you will never die. Those words may still sound strange to you. You may have never considered them in this way before, but this is God's truth. You will never die. Jesus Christ died your death; He tasted death to the full. He drank the cup, because of His great love for you.

We need not fear the end of our physical life. Our mortal will only be swallowed up in immortality. We will be transformed from glory to glory.

The more you look at grace, the more you will see God's love for you, and the more you will realize what our wonderful Lord has given us in His Son.

# Chapter 18

# The King's Friend

*"He who values grace and truth is the king's friend."*
**Proverbs 22:11 (The Living Bible)**

We are a little beyond the half-way mark in this book and at this time I would like to ask you a question. Do you value grace? Can you see the importance of grace in your life? Are you just reading a group of nice sounding meditations here, or are you receiving the Bread of Life?

I hope and pray this book is much more to you than simply an exercise in spiritual reading material. I trust you are finding the words I am sharing with you to be the *key* into the heart of God, and thus into abundant life. The reality is, in the same way an understanding of the finished work of Jesus Christ is the doorway into life eternal; so is an understanding of grace the doorway into an intimate and uniquely individual walk with God. Without an inner knowing concerning the power of grace, I'm afraid your perception of God will be dim at best.

Grace is the essence of God. Grace is the word which captures the what and why of all our Lord has accomplished for us.

Looking into grace is really looking into the very depths of the heart motivation of Jesus. The believer who attempts to grow spiritually, apart from grace, will always be approaching God on the basis of personal efforts or works. In other words, his Christian life will revolve around the externals, the obedience to commands. Without the knowledge of grace, those commands will make up a never ending list of demands.

Attempting to live in Christ without centering your life upon His grace is the same as telling God you're not really interested in knowing Him; you would rather keep Him at arms length, like the children of Israel when they told Moses to speak to God for them because they were afraid of His voice. This is spiritual double mindedness. On one hand you're telling God you want to serve Him and be all He wants you to be, and on the other hand you're ignoring the very power which would bring this to pass.

What is your desire as a Christian? Don't you want to know the Lord as deeply and intimately as you possibly can? Don't you want to be filled to the fullest with His love and power? Well, as I said, grace is the doorway to this life.

When Jesus spoke about abundant life, a joy made full, and about experiencing a peace which passeth all understanding, He wasn't exaggerating. What He said was exactly what He intended for us to have. However, I have counselled with thousands of Christians who have never known any of these blessings. Now either God is playing some spiritual cat and mouse game with us, or there is a fundamental lacking in what we are being taught concerning Jesus Christ. I have found the latter to be the sad truth.

There is simply a dearth of teaching concerning the grace of God. It seems everybody gets so excited about serving the Lord that they run off on pop teaching tangents and in the process leave

God behind. It's a classic case of zeal without knowledge, and the result is thousands of burned out believers who have worked their heads off to an accompanying sense of frustration as they begin to see themselves spinning their wheels and going nowhere.

As the Bible says, maybe it's time to be still and know He is God. Before you go running off, listen to what His will is. You will discover He hasn't called you to Himself for what He can extract from you in service to Him. Instead He called you, by name, to Himself that where He is, you might be also. Obedience does not produce spiritual growth. Rather, the knowing of your Savior in a progressive way, in an intimate way, will produce the obedience you desire to exhibit.

It's your choice. You can serve God as some unfathomable and distant Deity, or you can serve Him as His child, with a close Father-son relationship. You can go on striving to gain ground through your own efforts, or you can rest in His grace and really *know* abundant life, joy and peace.

I'm not advocating some course of laziness or indolence. What I'm speaking about is the realization of the kingdom of God which is within you, and from that experiential knowing, your course in life will be made clear. It's serving God out of what He has done, and who He is in you, rather than serving out of some mistaken concept that your works and efforts will bring you up to His level.

Without an intense valuing of God's grace, I'm afraid your Christianity will always be falling short of what you desire it to be. But if you do choose to honor and value grace, then you will be living in the throne room we spoke of earlier.

What I am sharing with you is put very well in the book of Proverbs. In the 11th verse of the 22nd chapter, the Scripture says, "He who values grace and truth is the king's friend" (The Living Bible). If you choose to focus your attention upon grace and truth, you will be growing in an understanding of the real nature of God, and you will always be close to Him. You will be the King's friend. But if instead you look at yourself, your works, your abilities, your faults, or any other thing, then you will not be coming close to God, and you won't experience the truth of being His friend.

To be, or not to be God's friend, this is the question. For many of you, this truth will be a confirmation from the Lord concerning something you had long felt must be the case. For others of you, what I'm sharing may be incredibly hard to accept because for so long you have heard the old guilt and condemnation messages which always focus their sights upon what you do. For you, it may be a case of letting the old things go in order to receive the glorious knowledge of a close relationship with the Lord through His grace.

If you value grace and truth, you will be the King's friend. God isn't picking who will be and who will not be His friends. He desires all His children to be His friends. It is we who are doing the picking and choosing in this case.

The Young's Literal Translation of the Bible puts the verse this way, "Whoso is loving cleanness of heart, Grace are his lips, a king is his friend." Jesus taught us that out of the abundance of the heart the mouth speaks. So if you love cleanness of heart, grace will be on your lips. A clean heart is filled with God's grace, and so the heart speaks grace. Grace is always on your lips, and the result is a king is your friend.

Jesus is your King, and grace is His nature. If grace is always on your lips, then this means you are always speaking of your friend, the King Jesus. The more you speak of Him in spirit and truth, the more you will be knowing Him, and the more your friendship will be deepening with Him. He in you, and you in He, will become your overwhelming reality.

Choosing to live in grace is the same as choosing to know the Lord as intimately as you possibly can. The more you grow, the more of His love you'll know, and the more you will value and cherish His grace.

# Chapter 19

# Stewards of Grace

*". . . if indeed you have heard of the stewardship of God's grace which was given to me for you."*          ***Ephesians 3:2***


*"As each one has received a special gift, employ it in serving one another as good stewards of the manifold grace of God."*
***1st Peter 4:10***


As we have seen, the grace of God is no matter to be taken lightly or passed over briefly. There is an inherit responsibility given us regarding grace. We are required to be stewards of this magnificent truth.

I believe one of the reasons Paul was so mightily used of the Lord was because of his commitment to truth. He didn't corrupt the Word of God with his own opinions. He wasn't prone to speak quickly concerning his own ideas. Today, quite the reverse seems to be the norm. How carelessly many handle the Word of God. There are whole segments of Christianity which seem to specialize in a particular word or phrase, as if their favorite teaching is more important than what the rest of the Bible has to say. This is not healthy and can only lead to a misunderstanding of Scripture.

Paul had grown up in strict adherence to the Jewish law. He had learned from an early age to painstakingly study Scripture, every jot and tittle. Regarding his years in Judaism, he once said, "If anyone has a mind to put confidence in the flesh, I far more: circumcised the eighth day, of the nation of Israel, of the tribe of Benjamin, a Hebrew of Hebrews; as to the law, a Pharisee; as to zeal, a persecutor of the church; as to the righteousness which is in the law, found blameless" (Philippians 3:4-6). Paul had taken much pride in his Judaism. It had been important for him to appear as an excellor next to his peers.

He learned of the futility he had been a slave of when God graciously gave him a new life. The church he once persecuted became the church he helped build. But in his new found relationship with God, he didn't forget to have a reverential regard for the Word, and God used this attribute of Paul's. He knew Paul would be a good steward of the mysteries of the Gospel, because Paul cared greatly for an accuracy of the truth.

We can see this trait throughout all of Paul's teaching, and he frequently admonished his children in the faith to maintain this same high regard for Scripture. To the Corinthians he said, ". . . that in us you might learn not to exceed what is written" (1st Corinthians 4:6). To his child in the faith, and apprentice, Timothy, he said, "be diligent to present yourself approved to God as a workman who does not need to be ashamed, handling accurately the word of truth" (2nd Timothy 2:15).

When we consider this, I think we can see why Paul was so diligent to speak time and time again of the grace of God. He knew this was the central truth to an understanding of the nature of

Jesus Christ, His finished work at Calvary, and our inclusion into the family of God. He knew the tendency of man, to take the gift of God and add his own embellishments to it, so he steadfastly held to and expounded upon grace.

God found an approved workman in the person of Paul, and so He entrusted the building of much of the early church to him, for the Lord knew Paul would always listen closely to His voice. He knew Paul wouldn't go off on some teaching tangent, or corrupt the message for selfish gain. Paul would be, and always was, a good and faithful steward who handled accurately the word of truth.

In his letter to the Ephesian church he said, " . . . if indeed you have heard of the stewardship of God's grace which was given to me for you" (3:2). When it came to the grace of God, Paul considered himself a steward of it. In other words he knew speaking of this truth was a great privilege and responsibility.

Webster's dictionary defines a steward as, "A person put in charge of a large estate." Do you know, when it comes to grace, we have been put in charge of a large estate? God's estate is called grace, and He has left it to us. The responsibility for us is to not disregard what He has placed us in charge of. In order to be a good steward of the estate, we must be continuously living in this great gift.

You have seen the vastness of grace in this book. I have shown you the powerful things grace has accomplished in your life. Now it is up to you to be a good steward of this grace. Care for it, live in it, prize it highly.

In the Gospel of Luke, Jesus gave us the parable of the faithful steward (Luke 12:35-48). In verse 42 of chapter 12, Jesus said, "Who then is the faithful and sensible steward, whom his master will put in charge of his servants, to give them their rations at the proper time? Blessed is that slave whom his master finds so doing when he comes. Truly I say to you, that he will put him in charge of all his possessions." Obviously, Jesus is exhorting His followers to be faithful stewards, and the incredible blessing is that the good steward will be put in charge of all of His possessions. Can you imagine that? Can you comprehend being put in charge of all of Christ's possessions? If you are willing to be a good and faithful steward, then this is exactly what will happen.

We know from the Word of God that we are to be faithful concerning God's grace. If we handle accurately the word of truth, of grace, then we will have a revelation of all of Christ's possessions which He has already granted us. It's as I said earlier, grace is the avenue, or open door, to an understanding of God's riches.

Before we leave this parable, there is one more truth I would like you to see. I almost missed it as I read this Scripture. I thought I knew what was being said, but as I looked more closely, I realized something quite different was coming forth. Starting at verse 35, the parable reads, "Be dressed in readiness, and keep your lamps alight. And be like men who are waiting for their master when he returns from the wedding feast, so that they may immediately open the door to him when he comes and knocks. Blessed are those slaves whom the master shall find on the alert when he comes; truly I say to you, that he will gird himself to serve, and have them recline at table, and will come up and wait on them." Upon my first reading, I scanned this passage thinking little of it, because I was mainly interested in the word, steward. But something caught my attention, so I went back and looked at it again. As I saw what Jesus was saying to us here, I was amazed. The passage which speaks of girding himself to serve and having them recline at table is not, as I originally assumed it was, referring to the slave. That passage is actually saying the master will serve the slave! Read it for yourself; that's what it says. When the master comes home to a good steward, the master will put on the loincloth, and serve the steward. That's almost too much to comprehend. All I can say is God must really value good stewards. In the Young's Literal Bible it says, " . . . he will gird himself, and will cause them to recline, and having come near, will minister to them." How would you like to have the Lord coming near and ministering to you? Well, according to this Scripture, we have it given to us in a perfectly understandable way. The truth is, if you will be a good steward, God will not only put you in charge of His possessions, but He will actually come near and minister to you.

Yes, being a steward is a high calling, but it also has high rewards. I don't know about you, but there are plenty of times when I desperately need a touch from God. I have many instances when I realize my own power or ability just isn't good enough; I need the Lord. Instead of crying out to God, and wondering if He will answer, wouldn't it be better to be acting as a good and faithful steward, with the inner assurance of God ministering to you?

Are you willing to accept the responsibility of being a steward? Are you willing to see this is God's word to you? If you don't respond to this call, I fear the blessings I have shared with you concerning grace will become as grains of sand trickling through your fingers. They will bless you as you read of them, but when you wake up tomorrow they will be gone from your mind, and you will once again be involved in the things which captivated your thoughts before. If you do receive this holy calling though, grace will become the estate you are in charge of, and the Lord Jesus Christ Himself will be personally ministering to you and making you aware of all His riches which are now in you.

Let me close this chapter with a word from the first epistle of Peter. In chapter 4, Peter is speaking to the believers about how the end of all things is at hand. In light of this fact he then says, "Be of sound judgment and sober spirit for the purpose of prayer. Above all, keep fervent in your love for one another, because love covers a multitude of sins. Be hospitable to one another without complaint. As each one has received a special gift, employ it in serving one another as good stewards of the manifold grace of God" (4:7-10).

Peter calls God's grace manifold in this passage. In other words, it is diverse. It has applications for many things. It is vast, and we are once again called to be good stewards of it. The Greek meaning of steward in this verse is to be a house-distributor or treasurer. If you were a treasurer for an organization, you would be in charge of the funds. The assets of your group would be under your care, and the members would come to you for the disbursement of the resources. So it is with God's grace. He has made you a treasurer of it, and according to this verse he wants you to be disbursing grace to those around you. This is another important meaning of being a steward. Not only are you in charge of the Lord's possessions, but you are also responsible to God to distribute these riches to His other servants.

To sum up; we must have a high regard for the grace which has been given us. We must be good and faithful stewards of it. We must remain in the household of grace at all times. We must be giving this grace to all around us. Being a good steward will bring us into the realization that God has distributed *all* of His riches to us experientially. We will also know He is in us, ministering to all our needs.

God is looking for people in this age who will diligently handle accurately the word of truth, even as His servant Paul did. God has a vast wealth to distribute and He is hoping to find good and faithful stewards through whom He will be able to make these riches known. Will you come forward and consecrate your heart to His service? Are you willing to become a good steward for the Lord?

It is not a matter of works, but of willingness. God is not looking at your efforts. He is looking upon your heart.

In Christ we have been given His will, His last testament. We have inherited all spiritual blessings and riches. Yet to so many, these are just words which have no real meaning. They mouth the statements about being rich in Christ while inwardly they are in anguish over the fact that they really do not experience these riches they are supposed to have. Grace, the essence and heart of God, which lives within us, is the key. As we become stewards of grace, we come into the realization that God has given all His assets into our hands. We are not beggers, we are disbursers. We have so much that we can't help but give it out.

Being a steward of God's grace is a responsibility, but it is also the inner knowing of abundance in Christ. Let us today joyously serve one another as good stewards of the manifold grace of God.

# Chapter 20

# Committed to Grace

*"And now I commend you to God and to the word of His grace, which is able to build you up and to give you the inheritance among all those who are sanctified."* **Acts 20:32**

In the last chapter we took a look at our stewardship of the grace of God. In this section, I would like to share with you about the two sides of commitment. This is similar to, yet distinct from, our study on stewardship.

Acts 15:40 says, "But Paul chose Silas and departed, being committed by the brethren to the grace of God."

How often have you read the book of Acts, or any book of the Bible for that matter, desiring to know what the main message is? The reason I ask this question is because I know how easy it is to dive into Scripture looking for one particular verse, or doctrine. We sometimes forget this is an entire book we are reading, with a center, or theme. The book of Acts, for instance, is about the establishment of the early church through the power of the Holy Spirit, the missionary journeys of the first few ministers, and of utmost importance, the Gospel they preached was the Gospel of

God's grace. This is the main message contained in the book of Acts. Yet I have seldom heard this expressed. What I hear instead usually dwells upon the miraculous side only, completely omitting the message which was delivered. Again, this touches upon handling accurately the word of truth.

A good way to study Scripture would be to read a book, or letter, all the way through. Keep in mind there were no verse or chapter divisions in the original manuscript. The book was written and meant to be taken as a whole. So read it this way a few times and then ask yourself, what is the main point being made? What is the thrust of the writer's teaching, the crux of the message? If you learn to study the Bible in this fashion, you will find Scripture making a lot more sense to you.

Getting back to Acts; the main message delivered by the apostles was the message of grace. Just get out a concordance, look up the references to the word grace in Acts, and you will find, upon studying these verses, that the references to grace make up the key thrust of the Gospel which was delivered.

So, verse 40 of chapter 15 tells us of Paul and Silas setting off on a missionary outreach together, and the Scripture says they were, "being committed by the brethren to the grace of God." As I consider this verse, I see two sides to the word commitment.

The first, and perhaps the more obvious of the two, is that grace was what Paul and Silas were committed to speaking of. They felt a holy obligation to tesitfy concerning the grace of God. They would not be swayed from grace, whether it meant being stoned and left for dead, or being worshipped as god's (see chapter 14). Circumstances and responses did not matter. What did matter was that they were called of the Lord to go forth ministering grace to the hearers, and they were committed to this goal.

The second meaning I see here is that as Paul and silas departed, the brethren committed them into the hands of God's grace. In other words they saw the grace of God as being able to protect the two brothers they were bidding farewell to. They knew if Paul and Silas were to stay in grace they would be staying in the heart of God, or under the shadow of His wings as the psalmist put it. There would be protection for them from all evils. Paul later wrote, in his second letter to the Corinthian church, that he experienced affliction on every side; conflicts without, fears within (7:5). It was only God's grace which upheld Paul. He knew the nature of the Lord. Others may have felt they could not be worthy of God if they ever expressed such feelings. They might have totally given up. But Paul knew even though he felt these fears and needed help, that God was a Lord of grace and would meet those very needs because He loved Paul and because Paul had been committed to the grace of God. Grace would always be there, to meet his every need.

There are two sides to commitment concerning the grace of God. You commit yourself to holding high the grace of God, and the grace of God commits itself to holding you high from all evil. To be committed to grace is your protection as well as your goal.

I would like to share a few more verses with you on this theme of commitment to grace and how it is a central message in the book of Acts.

In the 14th chapter of Acts, as Paul and Barnabas neared the close of their first missionary journey, the Scripture says, "And from there they sailed to Antioch, from which they had been commended to the grace of God for the work that they had accomplished" (verse 26). You see, from the very start, this had been the focus of their ministry.

While they were in the midst of this first outreach in Asia Minor, or the regions of Galatia as it was called then, we have this word given to us, "Many of the Jews and of the God-fearing proselytes followed Paul and Barnabas, who, speaking to them, were urging them to continue in the grace of God" (Acts 13:43). When they had originally left the church at Antioch, they had been commended, or committed, to the grace of God, and from this passage we can see they remained faithful to their calling.

Backing up even further, we have an account given to us in chapter 11. A persecution of the church had begun, which had stemmed from the martyrdom of Stephen, and this had resulted in a scattering of the believers. Some went to Phoenicia, others to Cyprus, and still others to Antioch. The early Christians, at this point in time, were confining their outreach to the house of Israel only. But verse 20 says, "There were some of them, men of Cyprus and Cyrene, who came to Antioch and began speaking to the Greeks also, preaching the Lord Jesus. And the hand of the Lord was with them, and a large number who believed turned to the Lord. And the news about them reached the ears of the church at Jerusalem, and they sent Barnabas off to Antioch." The apostles in Jerusalem were excited upon hearing this good news of the spreading of the Gospel, but I'm sure they were also concerned as to what message was being ministered. They wanted to make sure there was not a compromising or changing of the Gospel, so they dispatched Barnabas to look into the matter. The Scripture goes on to report, "When he had come and *witnessed the grace of God,* he rejoiced and began to encourage them all with resolute heart to remain true to the Lord" (verse 23). It is very clear here that remaining true to the Lord is synonymous with staying in the grace of God. What was it Barnabas saw which convinced him beyond any doubt that this was a genuine moving of the Spirit? He witnessed the grace of God among these gentile converts and for him, that was enough.

Later on, there was a critical moment in the early church. In the beginning, the first believers had all come from a Jewish background. However, as time went on the Holy Spirit began to be poured out upon all flesh, Jew and gentile. As we have just seen, those who truly loved the Lord rejoiced at this new development and fulfillment of prophecy. There were others though who viewed this situation through a critical eye. They were still stuck in the old covenant and so an important council was called in Jerusalem. These "Judaisers" were advocating adherence to the Mosiac law in addition to grace. In an earlier chapter we saw the danger of attempting to mix grace with anything else. This was a critical moment. The argument went back and forth for awhile, until at last Peter rose and addressed the assembly. He said, "Brethren, you know that in the early days God made a choice among you, that by my mouth the gentiles should hear the word of the Gospel and believe. And God, who knows the heart, bore witness to them, giving them the Holy Spirit, just as He also did to us; and He made no distinction between us and them, cleansing their hearts by faith. Now therefore why do you put God to the test by placing upon the neck of the disciples a yoke which neither our fathers nor we have been able to bear? But we believe that we are saved through the grace of the Lord Jesus, in the same way as they also are" (verses 7-11). After Peter; Paul, Barnabas, and James spoke on behalf of the grace of God too.

What is the message Peter delivered? Grace! Grace had saved them, and it was clear to Peter, grace would keep them. The law had been a burden, a yoke which no one could handle before and no one could handle now.

This was a pivotal stage, and grace won. It's important to realize that the same arguments are being raised against God's grace today, just as it was then. It is also important to realize the answer is still the same; grace and nothing but grace is what we are to live in and preach to the world. There will always be those who, out of their own personal ignorance and prejudice, will feel like grace is too simple, too free. They will feel the need to place restrictions upon believers, as if somehow God requires them to measure a Christian's commitment. They won't be able to let grace be grace. They will try to corrupt it. We must stand firmly against their attacks, in the same way Peter and the apostles stood against those who in their day tried to water down and change the Gospel of grace.

There is still one more instance I would like you to look at. This comes near the close of the Acts of the apostles. In chapter 20 we see Paul impressed by the Lord to return to Jerusalem even though he knows bonds and imprisonment awaited him. Some tried to dissuade him from this journey, but Paul knew what God had placed upon his heart, so on he went. His ship stopped briefly in Miletus, and Paul called for the elders of the Ephesian church to come meet with him. Paul knew this might be the last time he would ever see these beloved brothers of his, so he urgently warned them of the enemies of the Gospel. In verse 24, Paul spoke of his own fate. "But I do not consider my life of any account as dear to myself, in order that I may finish my course, and the ministry which I received from the Lord Jesus, to testify solemnly of the Gospel of the grace of God."

In all the intervening years, Paul had never once strayed from his commission. He had remained committed to the Gospel of the grace of God, and in this verse we see he considered the ministry of grace to be even more important than his own life. This is commitment. Paul's beginning had been grace, and as far as he was concerned, his end would be grace.

As he closed his exhortation to the Ephesian elders, he said, "And now I commend you to God and to the word of His grace, which is able to build you up and to give you the inheritance among all those who are sanctified" (verse 32).

We began this chapter with a verse revealing the twofold commitment which we encounter with grace, and now we see at the close of Paul's missionary work, the commitment and power of grace were just as real and relevant then as they had ever been.

Paul loved his brethren dearly. He had been their father in the Lord. He had watched them grow. He had seen their mistakes and failures, and he had been there to pick them up and point them once again to the grace of God. I'm sure this last coming together was a very painful and emotional time for Paul. His children had grown up. They were elders, and they were now ministering the Gospel as he had done to them so many years ago.

Paul may have worried, but he had seen one unfailing principle which had always upheld him, even in his darkest moments, and he knew he could entrust his own dear children in the faith to the Lord, because he knew the grace which had always sustained him would also be more than abundant to protect his brethren. So, he commended them to God and to the word of His grace.

Having seen all this, I hope you will have deep in your heart this same commitment to the grace of God. I pray you will commend yourself to grace, making this message paramount in your own life, and I pray also you will realize the commitment of grace to you. God will always be there, whether you are on the highest mountaintop praising His name, or in the deepest valley full of fear. It doesn't matter, for once you commit yourself to the grace of God, you set the seal on an unbreakable bond between you and your Savior.

# Chapter 21

# Grace is Sufficient

*"My grace is sufficient for you, for power is perfected in weakness."*                    **2nd Corinthians 12:9**

The more you grow, the weaker you get. How does this statement sound to you? It seems to be a contradiction of what you should believe. According to the world, a saying like that would be a contradiction of growth. We think of growth primarily in regard to our bodies. As far as we're concerned, growth and development usually means becoming stronger. The more a tree grows, the stronger it gets. The more a country grows, the more powerful it becomes. So, to say the more you grow, the weaker you get would certainly seem wrong.

But, I am speaking of the kingdom of God and not the kingdom of this world. When I say the more you grow, the weaker you get, I'm speaking of one of the mysteries of God.

I have met many a brother in the Lord who, after being saved a short time, feels as if he has God's word for everyone. He assumes he is strong. He is ready to do anything and everything.

I have counselled with thousands of Christians who cannot

understand why they are unable to conquer their own faults. They say they got off to a good start but, after awhile that fault got the best of them. They are confused and they feel like they must have let the Lord down.

Other believers I have talked to are completely frustrated in their Christian life. They are living contradictions. What they preach and proclaim they are unable to live.

The answer to these situations is simple. Each one of these people have not learned the secret of what I call "growing weakness." Why is the first brother so sure of himself and so presumptuously speaking? He is relying upon his own strength and thoughts. Why are these other Christians unable to conquer their own faults even though they had some initial success? They have trusted their own strength and thoughts. Their own power was good for awhile but, will power always loses to the power of sin. Why are these other believers so frustrated? They are trusting in their own strength and thoughts.

All of these situations happen frequently, because we are used to living in a world system where the principle of growth is; the more you grow, the stronger you get. When we enter the kingdom of God, there are new rules we must learn and, in many cases, this means unlearning the old rules. We must understand how meager our own thoughts are. God says, "My thoughts are not your thoughts, neither are your ways My ways, declares the Lord. For as the heavens are higher than the earth, so are My ways higher than your ways, and My thoughts than your thoughts" (Isaiah 55:8&9).

There is a new way of thinking which we must learn, and this new way is based upon communing with God in our spirit. God's truth does not become reality through our mental process. His truth is something He gives to us through our spirits. A mind which is dedicated to the Lord will learn much, but in that dedication there should be an accompanying knowledge of how limited our minds really are.

How long is eternity? What is on the other side of the universe? If God has always been, how did He get there? Who can answer these questions? Try to and you will very soon have an experience in which your mind simply reaches its end and can go no further. Our thoughts are finite. God is infinite. We have time and space boundaries. God has none.

We have to learn a whole new way of living. The trouble with so many believers today is that they are trying to fit Christianity into the constructs of this world where growth is strength, bigger is better, and spirituality is defined by external manifestations rather than through a renewing of the mind. We are the people of God, "a chosen race, a royal priesthood, a holy nation, a people for God's own possession" (1st Peter 2:9). As this royal priesthood, we have to develop the sense of our spirit in hearing the voice of God. Waiting upon the Lord and ministering unto His name are to be the qualities of our new created beings. Instead of "trying to live", we need to release ourselves from our efforts. It is Christ who now lives His life in us.

In Paul's letter to the Galatian churches he said, "The Gospel which was preached by me is not according to man. For I neither received it from man nor was I taught it, but I received through a revelation of Jesus Christ" (1:11&12). This revelation process Paul speaks of indicates a new way of learning things. His Gospel was not systematically explained to him, neither did he think it through on his own. He received it by having an open heart to God.

Haven't you ever experienced being in a difficult situation where you had allowed yourself to get agitated and frustrated beyond control? In the midst of your diverse thoughts a Scripture comes to mind, or a gentle impression is given from the Holy Spirit, and your inner tempest is stilled. This is receiving the things of God. It's an example of His ways and how they are higher than your ways and thoughts.

In his first letter to the Corinthian church, Paul elaborates on this theme. In chapter 2 he wrote, "We have received, not the spirit of this world, but the spirit who is from God, that we might know the things freely given to us by God." Here he establishes the two avenues of learning. You can incline your mind and heart to the spirit of this world or you can, by faith, entrust yourself to the Spirit of God.

Continuing on, Paul says, "Which things we also speak, not in words taught by human wisdom, but in those taught by the Spirit, combining spiritual thoughts with spiritual words. But a natural man (one who does not know Christ) does not accept the things of the Spirit of God; for they are foolishness to him, (as in the case of the more you grow, the weaker you get) and he cannot understand them, because they are spiritually appraised" (2:12-14). In order for us to grow spiritually in any significant way, we will have to begin learning through the spirit, and we must discard the old natural way of doing things. Unless we are willing to let go, the new wine will not be poured, because new wine must go into a new wineskin.

One fundamental principle of the Spirit is; the more we grow, the weaker we become. You will find this quality deeply implanted in the hearts of those who have walked closely with their Lord for a number of years. There is a reluctance in these saints to speak opinion. There is a heavy dependence upon the Lord for all things; not just the large things, but all things.

When John the Baptist was told of the widespread following Jesus was acquiring, he simply replied, "He must increase, but I must decrease" (John 3:30). This is exactly what I am speaking of. In order to grow, there must be an increase of the awareness of Jesus in our lives. Many Christians would readily agree with this statement, but I am not finished. There must be an increase of Jesus in our lives, and it must be matched with a decrease of our own self-reliance. Most believers will assent to the need of more of Jesus, but how many will say as quickly that there needs to be a lessening of self? As we follow the Lord, we will begin to understand how worthless our own strength is.

We often hear of the necessity for our faults and weaknesses to be brought to the cross of Christ, but I want to tell you, this is not scriptural. Nowhere in the Bible are we told that our bad parts must go to the cross. No, the Bible requires the whole man to be identified with Jesus at Calvary, and this means our so-called good qualities as well as the ones we are willing to see as detrimental. You may think your own self-control is something to be proud of, but I tell you unless your self-control dies at the cross, it will inhibit your growth in Christ. God wants to deal with your self-control, which is imperfect, bring it to the cross, and replace it with His self-control. God wants to take your strength to serve Him, and crucify it with Christ, so His strength to serve may be realized in you.

When we see and receive this purpose of God in our lives, then we will gladly say, "The more I grow, the weaker I become" because the weaker you become in yourself, the stronger He becomes in you.

I have a personal love for Paul's second Corinthian letter, for in it he reveals his own faults, fears, and weaknesses, and this is something I can identify with. He doesn't speak of these things in a self-deprecating way though. Rather, he shares how he learned the great principle of God's strength through his weaknesses.

In chapter 12, Paul tells us of a thorn which was given to him. Because of the great revelations he had seen, this thorn was given him to keep him from exalting himself. Three times he asked the Lord to remove the thorn. You may think, as I'm sure Paul thought, that he would be hindered from his service to Christ if the thorn remained. You see, that's the old way of thinking. We feel any trial or thorn in our flesh limits us, because we are still thinking in terms of *our* ability, and not the Lord's ability in us.

God did not remove Paul's thorn, for he had something important to tell Paul. After his third time in prayer, Paul was ready to hear the message.

By this time, it began to dawn upon him, that maybe it was not God's will to remove this thorn. I'm sure Paul originally assumed that God wanted the thorn to go. When he was ready to hear, God spoke, "My grace is sufficient for you, for power is perfected in weakness" (verse 9). That word struck Paul like a thunderbolt. It ran contrary to all he naturally assumed. But when God spoke the word, light dawned and Paul was a changed man. What joy there was in that simple declaration of God.

Paul had striven in prayer. He had tried all he could to remove the thorn. But as the depth of the Lord's word was realized, I'm sure a sweet peace and comfort came over the apostle. God did not require Paul to be some spiritual superman. God wasn't honored by strength of the flesh. On the contrary, He was limited by Paul's own natural resources.

Grace is sufficient for you! Are you fighting some sin single handed? Grace is sufficient for you. Are you in turmoil over your work for the Lord? Grace is sufficient for you. Do you need a miracle in your life? Grace is sufficient for you.

Arkëō is the Greek word used for sufficient in this verse and it means to be enough. No matter what trial, tribulation, or affliction faces you, God has supplied enough grace to carry you through. Grace is always sufficient to the occasion.

Can you confess that grace is sufficient for you, or do you still need to learn the lesson concerning your own strength? The more you grow, the weaker you get, so that God can become stronger in you. Perhaps you have been wrestling with the Lord over some thorn in your own life. It is now time to stop fighting. Let God speak His word of grace to you. Rest in the finished work of Jesus Christ, and watch His grace carry you where you could never have gone on your own strength or ability.

Christian, it doesn't matter what life throws at you, because God's grace is sufficient for you. It always will be. No matter how big you think grace is, I can tell you it is still bigger. There will always be enough grace for you, and as you learn to listen with your spirit to the voice of God, you will find His grace being magnified more and more in you. God's power is perfected in your weakness, because His grace is what makes you all you desire to be as His child. His grace is sufficient for you!

# Chapter 22

# Grace to the Humble

*"God is opposed to the proud, but gives grace to the humble"*
*James 4:6, Proverbs 3:34, 1st Peter 5:5*

I frequently receive a particular question on my live call-in-counselling radio program. The question is "How do I know when I'm hearing God's voice? How can I tell the difference between my voice, God's voice, and Satan's voice?" My usual reply to the person who asks this question is, "You have already made the first, all important, step in being able to distinguish God's voice from other voices." This brings a startled reply of how can this be? As far as that person can see, he has not taken any step. If anything, he may even feel he is less likely to hear God's voice than others.

The reason why I say that person has taken the first step is because I have found the one who realizes how easily he could be mistaken is most likely the very one who will be able to distinguish between the voice of his own mind from that of the mind of the Lord. The inner awareness of how weak he is, is the very thing which will cause him to listen all the more closely.

On the other hand, I have found the one who assumes every

thought which comes into his mind must be a word from the Lord has the dangerous tendency to speak nothing but his own opinions and feelings, and he usually adds a "Thus saith the Lord" to the end of every idea of his. This person doesn't think he can make a mistake. He assumes he knows everything about everything, and those who are of a different mind must be spiritually inferior to him. The result is this person tries to minister the Lord, but instead he ministers death to the hearers for he has not learned to tell the difference between his mind and the mind of Christ.

The first person will learn, through trial and error, how to tell the difference between God's voice and his own. He will understand there is no instant formula for this situation. There is only yieldedness and a commitment to follow the Lord moment by moment, learning as He teaches.

Unfortunately, I have heard many a sad tale of some church which was growing in the Lord being torn apart by some so called prophet. Some self appointed individual who can't tell his judgmental opinions from the compassion of God, tries to take over a congregation so he can exercise authority over the individual members. Nothing quenches the sweet Spirit of the Lord quicker than some power hungry and flesh controlled believer.

This person has also never learned the lesson of how useless his own thoughts are to God. The root of these situations is pride.

I believe Satan's main weapon in destroying congregations is pride. He will gladly whisper in someone's ear that they are one of the two olive branches the book of Revelation speaks of. The devil knows if a person swallows that lie, they will quickly leave the place of dependence upon God and they will run off after their own visions of grandeur. If the particular group doesn't have enough wisdom, in a short while they will all be trying to out prophesy each other. Where once the Lord Jesus Christ was Head, there will be instead a competitive spirit of external spirituality. Pride indeed causes a great fall.

A person in that condition will never learn of God's grace, because he will be too busy trusting his own sufficiency. His pride in his own wisdom and strength will blind him from the grace of Jesus.

There is a Scripture from the book of Proverbs which is quoted twice in the New Testament. It is, "God is opposed to the proud, but gives grace to the humble" (James 4:6, Proverbs 3:34, 1st Peter 5:5). As we have seen, God is opposed to pride because pride keeps us from receiving the things of the Lord. Pride is a subtle deception, for the one caught in its snare truly believes himself to be spiritual.

However, the one who abhors pride is the open vessel for the Master's use, and he doesn't consider himself, in his flesh, as anything. He has no need to regard himself for he is identified with and in Jesus Christ.

Humility is not, as some mistakenly claim, self deprecation. That is only pride in reverse. The one who considers hemself as something great, and the one who thinks he is a nothing or a worm, are both caught in the grip of pride. Pride, at its base, is self-consciousness. True humility is Christ consciousness. If you are always putting yourself down, you are the same as the one who struts arrogantly about. You are caught in a self fixation, and that is pride.

God gives grace to the humble because only the humble are listening. The proud self produced spiritual one is too enamored with his own qualities. The proud self abasing one is too busy recounting his faults or the wrongs done to him. Neither of these people will see grace as long as they allow, and therefore encourage, their hearts to remain in the state of pride.

Humility is not something you try to achieve. When you begin leaning upon the Lord in all things, you will be humble. You don't produce humility. Humility comes about as you fix your eyes on Jesus, the Author and Finisher of your faith. Look to Jesus and you will be humble. Look to yourself and you will be proud. If you try to achieve a state of humility on your own, you will only be fortifying pride's hold upon your life.

God gives grace to the humble. According to the Greek word, tapĕinŏs, humble means depressed, humiliated, cast down, and lowly. As I have already pointed out, this depression is not a hung up on self cast down state. Rather it is as Jesus said when He declared, "Blessed are the poor in spirit, for theirs is the kingdom of heaven" (Matthew 5:3). We are to be cast down and lowly regarding our own necessity for Christ in all things. We are to be humiliated when we see our arrogant attempts at producing growth for what they are, pride. We are to be depressed in the sense of being pressed down before the Lord at the cross.

Even our Lord said, "The Son can do nothing of Himself" (John 5:19). Jesus knew He was not here to simply do and say whatever struck His fancy. He came to do God's will and He was utterly dependent upon receiving input from His heavenly Father. As Paul later wrote to the Philippians, "And being found in appearance as a man, He humbled Himself by becoming obedient to the point of death, even death on a cross" (2:8).

Jesus was not caught in a self centered pride. On the contrary, He was wholly consumed with doing the Father's will. This is true Biblical humility and this is why John wrote that grace and truth were realized in Jesus Christ (John 1:17).

God gives grace to the humble. If you truly desire to know all you can about the glorious grace of God, then allow God to be your all sufficiency. Fix your heart and mind upon Jesus, and you will find grace abounding in your life.

# Chapter 23

# Grace is Abounding

*"And God is able to make all grace abound to you, that always having all sufficiency in everything, you may have an abundance for every good deed."*      *2nd Corinthians 9:8*

*"For all things are for your sakes, that the grace which is spreading to more and more people may cause the giving of thanks to abound to the glory of God."*

*2nd Corinthians 4:15*

The beautiful truth you will soon discover about grace is, the more you look into it with understanding, the more it will continue to grow in you. Grace will always be larger than your capacity to comprehend it. We saw in an earlier chapter that we will be looking into grace for all eternity, and this can only mean grace is inexhaustible! Paul said, " . . . in order that in the ages to come He might show the surpassing riches of His grace in kindness toward us in Christ Jesus" (Ephesians 2:7). God's grace has always been given to us in kindness. In other words, because God loves us so much, He has given grace to us and, as the verse indicates here, God loves us all so much that grace will be given to us throughout all eternity. He may have many other riches to reveal to us, but when it comes to grace, Paul calls it "surpassing riches". The riches of grace surpass all else.

This truth has many applications. First, if we will be given new revelations concerning grace throughout all eternity, then it only makes perfect sense to be steadfastly gazing into grace right now. Second, if grace is what God wants to reveal to His children in eternity, then shouldn't we, as His ambassadors, be telling the world about His grace now? And third, if grace will always be increasing, then doesn't this have a special meaning for our daily lives now? Can we trust God to give us an increasing awareness of grace in our lives right now, to meet any and every circumstance?

I believe the answer to all these questions is yes. Let us not wait till eternity comes before we begin living in the grace of God. Let us begin now. Let's look into the riches of grace, proclaim to the world God's grace in kindness, and let's see grace become enlarged in our own personal lives.

Don't make the mistake of putting off God's riches to some future date. Live in them now, for this is His will concerning you.

In his letter to the church at Rome, Paul wrote, "For if by the transgression of the one, death reigned through the one, much more those who receive the abundance of grace and of the gift of righteousness will reign in life through the one, Jesus Christ" (5-17). This teaching is very clear. Grace is more abundant than death or sin. We have seen both of these truths in earlier chapters, but we are looking at them again from the perspective of the abundance of grace. Grace is so abundant, so great, that it delivers us from sin and death. I don't know about you, but if grace is this powerful in my life, then I'm going to keep my focus upon it. How often Christians fall into the trap of looking at the sin which tries to pull them down. Sin won't save you, but grace will deliver you. Look at grace, not at sin, and you will be experiencing God's hand of power lifting you above your circumstances. Grace is more than abundant every time.

Pĕrissĕia is the Greek word used for abundance in this verse, and it literally means, superabundance! As we choose by faith to walk in God's grace, we are actually availing ourselves of our Lord's superabundance. If we were to say there was an abundance of grace for every situation, we would be meaning that grace was more than enough to carry us through that trial or difficulty. But even this is not the whole truth, for the fact of the matter is, we have a superabundance. Not just more than enough, but so much more that we couldn't possibly ever fathom it.

We have unseen riches and power at our fingertips. Not riches as some teach; as if you can command God to be your servant and do for you whatever you want. The riches I'm speaking of is the abundance of grace which is in us in the person and nature of our Lord Jesus Christ, and this abundance will deliver us out of the hand of the enemy every time. When we see this great abundance, this superabundance, we can rest in the arms of our Savior. Jesus is in us. Grace is His being. There is so much grace in Him, and therefore in us, that we can know He is continually bringing us safely through all things.

Try this simple exercise. Take some difficulty you are facing now and say to it, "The superabundance of grace in me is more than enough to give me the victory in this trial. I rest in the finished work and love of my Savior." If you can truly declare this, then you have chosen to live according to the kingdom of

God. You have surpassed this world's way of doing things, you have touched resurrection life in Jesus, and you will witness the power of grace as you rest in His glory. You may be surrounded by those who will have absolutely no idea what you are doing, but you will know, because you will be experiencing the riches of His grace in kindness.

The point is, if we truly believe God's grace is superabundant, then we ought to live as if it really is. The worst deception we can live in is to confess the truth of God's word, and then go on with our lives as we always have, relying upon our own thoughts and reactions. This nullifies the power of God, and lulls us into a false sense of spirituality. We need to be courageous and look for opportunities to let God's grace be our abundance, our all sufficiency. If we will, then God's truth will become reality in our lives. Remember, we are to live to the Lord, not man.

To try and convince those around you that you possess understanding is futile. Live unto the Lord. Don't talk about what you know. Live what you know, and all will be convinced. Live what you know, and you will continually be discovering the closeness which exists in your relationship with the Lord.

In his second letter to the Corinthian church, Paul got into the matter of giving. People in that day were just the same as people today. The problem was that they were living as if their only possessions were those things which they could see with their eyes and touch with their hands. So their giving was affected, for the worse. There was a great need among the churches in the Judean area. Famine had struck and people were in desperate need of food. Paul was attempting to raise funds to meet this need, but he was encountering a dragging of the feet in the Corinthian church. They were looking at the situation through their own eyes and they were ignoring God's perspective.

In chapter 9, Paul wrote, "Now this I say, he who sows sparingly shall also reap sparingly; and he who sows bountifully shall also reap bountifully" (verse 6). Simply put, our self-determined capacity to give will become our capacity to receive. If you live in the kingdom of God, and give of yourself accordingly, then you will also receive great things. But, if you are narrow and hold back from giving, then you will be holding back from receiving as well. We are spiritual conduits. The more we give, the more we enable ourselves to receive.

In the next verse, Paul said, "Let each one do just as he has purposed in his heart; not grudgingly or under compulsion; for God loves a cheerful giver." When we learn to live out of our hearts instead of our heads, then we are truly availing ourselves of the riches of Christ. Our heads will always find reasons not to give. Our hearts will always be moved with compassion. Our heads make decisions apart from the Lord. Our hearts are in touch with God. Our heads say "my will". Our hearts say "Thy will". When we learn to do as we have purposed in our hearts, we begin living in the abundance of grace.

If we learn this, then Paul's next statement will be reality for us. He said, "And God is able to make all grace abound to you, that always having all sufficiency in everything, you may have an abundance for every good deed." You see, in our own natural thinking we assume that to give means we suffer loss. This is not true, for God sees our giving heart and He always gives greater back to us. God is a giving God and He is looking for children with giving hearts, for the one who gives is saying, "I want to be as my Lord who has given so much to me." To give means we are living beyond ourselves. It means we believe what the Bible says about our riches in Christ, and it means we are actively seeking the abundance of grace.

Look at it this way. Do you really want to see the abundance of grace in your own life? Well, God has a promise here and the promise is, when we learn to live and give from our hearts, God will give to us so that we will experientially know the abounding of grace in our lives.

God will make all grace abound to us! Paul goes on to define what this will mean to us in our daily lives. He tells us we will always have a sufficiency in everything. In other words, we will not suffer any lack. If we live with our eyes only fixed in this world, then we will most certainly suffer a lack of things. But if we learn to live in the grace of God, we will always have a sufficiency for everything. Paul continues by saying we will also have an abundance for every good deed. Because we chose to fix our eyes upon Jesus in this manner, we will be living in the mind of Christ, so we will be ready in any situation to give as the Lord would have us give.

So much of what I call "Pop Christianity" revolves around what you can get. It's an extremely self-centered religion, and that alone makes it the antitheses of what Jesus came to do. Jesus came giving, and yet these self proclaimed experts of the Word would have you believe all that matters today is getting. It's a very selfish getting.

God is not against your receiving His promises and riches. On the contrary, He desires you to know these things. He came to us giving and He wants us to receive what He has given. But there is something fundamentaly wrong when a Christian believes receiving is simply a matter of claiming some specific promise. The Scriptures are emphatic upon this subject. We receive as we give. Our giving heart is the product of God's gift to us. The one who does not give is only declaring he has not been touched by the Lord. If you have truly received something from God, you will be changed. You will not be into Christianity for what you can get out of it. You will be transformed from a self-centered person to a Christ-centered giving person. Your world will no longer revolve around yourself, but you will know of God's great forgiveness to you and this will create a capacity for you to love much.

"Pop Christianity" has a naturally understandable appeal. It's an ear-tickling theology. There are no requirements placed upon you except for you to know. Real Christianity, however, has a cross at the center. There is receiving, but it is in resurrection life which follows the Cross. When a person has truly been to the Cross, then he knows what he has, but he also has been conformed into the image of Christ. There is no more room for self-centeredness.

It is in this context that Paul speaks of knowing the superabundance of grace in our lives. Grace is more real than anything in this world, but we are not to callously sit and gloat over our riches, for a true understanding of grace means we see the need to be living moment by moment in the mind of Christ. As we give, God causes His grace to abound towards us so that our every need is met.

This knowledge of the interwoven truth of giving and receiving was evident in Paul's own personal life. Earlier on in 2nd Corinthians he said, "So death works in us, but life in you" (4-12).

Paul had been writing about all the afflictions he had suffered as he served the Lord. In this verse he shares where his heart was concerning this. He was not bitter. He wasn't walking about with a chip on his shoulder. He wasn't harboring a grudge against God. On the contrary, we know he counted it a privilege to suffer as His Lord had suffered. Paul knew that being identified with Christ in his pain meant he would also be identified with Him in resurrection (see Philippians 3:10). So the apostle said, "death works in us, but life in you."

As he gave of himself, he knew he would be receiving more grace and therefore, he would be a more capable minister to those around him. This is, in fact, one of the main themes of his second Corinthian letter. It is also important to know what Paul thought of this cross and resurrection relationship. Down in verse 17 he wrote, "For momentary light affliction is producing for us an eternal weight of glory far beyond all comparison." The sufferings of this life, which came about as a result of his commitment to Jesus Christ, could not even be compared to the glory he was receiving. Here is a flesh and blood testimony concerning the superabundance of grace.

When Paul spoke of his hardships, was he admitting defeat? No, he was really saying these afflictions were the very tool and avenue to the reception of more riches. God's grace was always more than abundant.

In the 15th verse, Paul wrote, "For all things are for your sakes, that the grace which is spreading to more and more people may cause the giving of thanks to abound to the glory of God." Paul had the giving heart. He had been transformed and he knew the secret of the abundant grace which was his in Jesus Christ. He knew the glory of God's increasing grace in his own life, and the sign that he truly understood this was expressed in his desire to be giving of himself so others would know grace as well. He saw the things he received not in a shallow selfish light, but he saw them as being for others.

Once again, we see the connection between grace and abundance. Becaue of Paul's yieldedness to the Lord, grace was not only abounding in his own life, but it was spreading to more and more people, with the result that many were giving thanks to God.

Grace has, inherent within itself, the quality of abundance. Grace is not some finite inanimate object, it is more like a spiritual organism which keeps on growing. In order to grow, it needs to be placed within a human heart.

When you connect with God's grace, an abundance of grace is discovered. This grace keeps abounding in you as you look more fully into it. Ultimately there is a kind of spiritual explosion, and grace comes running out of you to the world around you. Grace keeps abounding and overflowing in you and out of you. This is why we will always be seeing the riches of grace in kindness throughout all eternity. Grace is so big that it defies a complete description. We can only hope to catch a glimpse of its true meaning.

I realize I have shared a great deal with you in this book about grace, but I also have an accompanying knowledge that I am simply scratching the surface of this magnificent truth. There is so much more to know. As we live each day, with our eyes fixed upon Jesus, we will be increasing in the knowledge of grace. We will continue to see the superabundance of grace in our lives, but we will also always carry in us the realization that there is so much more to know. One million years from now we will declare, "There is so much more to know."

Grace abounds. Grace is more powerful than any other spiritual principle because it is always abounding. It is never stagnant.

We know grace is the nature of God. Well, think of God's nature as an expanding universe. It's always growing, so we will always be growing throughout eternity, because God's nature and grace will always be expanding and increasing throughout all eternity.

There is certainly more than enough grace for your life right now. Receive His grace. Watch it grow in you, and watch it grow out of you to the point that the world is being touched and transformed because of the abundance of grace found in your own life.

# Chapter 24

# Stand and Be Strong in The Grace of God

*"Do not be carried away by varied and strange teachings; for it is good for the heart to be strengthened by grace."*

**Hebrews 13:9**

*"You therefore, my son, be strong in the grace that is in Christ Jesus."* **2nd Timothy 2:1**

*". . . Through whom also we have obtained our introduction by faith into this grace in which we stand."* **Romans 5:2**

*"I have written to you briefly, exhorting and testifying that this is the true grace of God. Stand firm in it!"*

**1st Peter 5:12**

In this world, to be strong means to possess great natural ability. A strong person is regarded as one who has physical prowess, intelligence, fame, or financial power. Sometimes we refer to a determined person as having a strong personality. "Charisma" is another word we use in describing someone who has a magnetic attraction upon people regarding his own ideas or causes.

This is strength in the world's eyes, but for the Christian strength comes from quite a different quarter. A believer's strength is not of himself. It's not a matter of willing something into being. Rather, it is a case of looking beyond ourselves to the "rock that is higher than I" (Psalm 61:2).

A minister who tries to convince people that real spiritual strength comes from some inner resolve or awareness of his own power, is simply misleading his listeners. I've counselled with many a Christian who mistakenly assumed God required him to develop an inner fortitude by his own resolve. The sad consequence of allowing such thoughts to reside in his conscience is failure and frustration. There is no way you can make your own strength into God's strength and, most importantly, God has never asked you to that anyway.

There are those who pride themselves upon their own ability. They subconsciously take the credit for what God accomplishes in their lives. They might testify of how great the Lord is, but when you listen to them why do you come away with the feeling that they are more spiritual and powerful than you are? It's because they really were saying, "You just make up your mind, claim your answer, and God will come through for you." Who is responsible for the results in that type of theology; the God who did it or the you who claimed it? All too often you are made to feel that *self* performed the victory; God merely responded to what you commanded. In other words, the Lord played a supporting role while ego held the center stage.

This type of self-centered Christianity confuses the issue of trusting God. You are made to feel that the burden of an answer from the Lord is dependent upon you rather than upon Him. Your faith becomes the central issue and God's power is pushed into the background. Furthermore, faith becomes totally redefined in this theology. Instead of a simple hope and trust in God's love and ability, you are told real faith is when you take some Scripture (usually by wrenching it out of context), and demand God to perform the specific results you require of Him. It is inconceivable to me how any person could think it admirable to treat God in this way. It's amazing that some people actually believe God is pleased when His children order Him around like some servant. Moreover, I have a hard time justifying this description of faith when I look at Jesus Christ and the lives of those who were martyred for their faith in Him.

Can you see the subtlety of human nature here? Can you see how we impose our own interpretations of strength in the issue and thus come away with something the Bible never intended? Our value of our own strength and ability is so important to us that we can change the whole thrust of God's power just so we can claim a piece of the action. The idea of real spiritual strength being a quality which is completely seperate from us is simply something which many will not accept.

We have seen in earlier chapters that when we are weak, we are really strong, because God's power can come into being when there is a willingness to trust completely in Him. Many times it is not until we abandon the principle of natural strength that God's true strength is able to be revealed.

Spare yourself from the thinly veiled attempts at redefining faith as some excuse to take the credit for God's power. Release yourself from the burden of thinking God can't do anything until you command Him to do so. In that environment you will always be thwarting His purpose in you, and you will also be filled with guilt and confusion every time something doesn't happen in the way you claimed it. You'll feel your faith must not be up to par. Let me make a simple statement regarding faith. Real faith points you to Jesus. Pseudo faith points you to self. Real faith makes you aware of God's power. False faith zeros in on your own ability, or as the case many times turns out, your lack of ability.

Now that we have clearly seen where true strength comes from, let's devote the rest of this chapter to seeing how this Godly strength can be made manifest in our lives.

At the close of his epistle, the writer of Hebrews said, "Do not be carried away by varied and strange teachings; for it is good for the heart to be strengthened by grace" (13:9). As we have just seen, it is so easy for us to be carried away. The reason why we are so quickly led astray lies in our Adamic nature. In the same way we redefine faith, we also redefine and change all of Christianity Our old natural hearts love hearing some particular preachment that purports to be the secret to spiritual life, victory, and power. We just love thinking we can learn some doctrine which puts all of God's promises (and even some new promises) at our disposal. At the heart of every varied and strange teaching is *self* thinking it can do what only God can do. Whether it be pin-pointing the date of the second coming and the identity of the beast, or adopting the stance that every sin can be instantaneously overcome by a deliverance session, or by believing speaking in tongues is the key to all spirituality, or discipleship, authority, or any other thing, it all revolves around self producing the results by adhering to and learning the particular teaching that is espoused. The result is; Christ is pushed out of the center and the doctrine occupies primary importance. A living realtionship is exchanged for theological understanding.

The only way to combat our never-ending tendency to stray from a Christ-centered life back into a self-centered life is found in letting our hearts be strengthened by grace. Grace will always point us to God. Grace is the one area where self simply cannot take any credit. Grace is all Jesus. If we allow ourselves to be strengthened by grace, we will be spared from running down many perilous dead ends. Varied and strange teachings will have no appeal for us because we have tasted and have seen that the Lord is good.

Once you tap into the fullness of God as it is revealed in grace, nothing else will ever satisfy. You will be free from the folly of thinking God can be fully defined and understood by some one-answer-fits-all teaching. Grace will make your heart strong so that you won't be misled. It's as they say, once you have the real thing, you will never be fooled by a counterfeit again. Grace *is* the real thing.

There is strength in grace. Not some self produced strength, but real Godly strength. Grace makes you strong because it points you to Jesus. He is your strength and He is in you as your life. Grace puts you into the heart of God, and when you're there you won't be misled. It's as Jesus once said, referring to Himself as the Good Shepherd, "The sheep follow him because they know his voice. And a stranger they simply will not follow, but will flee from him, because they do not know the voice of strangers" (John

10:4&5). When you choose to live in God's grace, every other voice will be a strange voice and you simply will not listen to it. So, you see, there is strength in grace. Grace keeps you true in the Lord. Grace spares you from all varied and strange teachings. Let your heart be saturated with grace today and you will be protecting yourself from all false doctrines.

In the second letter to his child in the faith, Timothy, Paul said, "You therefore, my son, be strong in the grace that is in Christ Jesus" (2nd Timothy 2:1). Paul had a lot of hard words for Timothy in this letter. He knew if Timothy was going to be effective in his ministry, then he would have to be willing to follow Jesus at all costs. He told him to suffer hardship with him (verse 3), to be a soldier (verse 4), to be a competing athlete (verse 5), and to be as a hard working farmer (verse 6).

It is significant to note that prior to these consecutive exhortations, his word to Tomothy was to be strong in the grace that is in Christ Jesus. Paul knew Timothy would never be able to be any of these things unless he first chose to be strong in grace. Grace is real power. If Timothy trusted in his own resolve and ability, he would fail. But, if he would trust in the Lord, placing his complete reliance upon God's power, then he would indeed be all these things.

We desperately need to understand that grace is the only power and strength which is worth considering. Anything else will be the same old song of mixing grace and works, which we have already seen is a complete farce.

It's like being a television set. We will never get the picture unless we get plugged into the power supply. The T.V. has all it needs in it to work, but the power to make it work comes from an external source. So it is with us. We have everything in us to be completely victorious. We have been given all spiritual blessings. We are joint-heirs with Christ. But none of these things will experientially do us any good unless we get plugged into our source. Our power supply is 100% Jesus and His power lives in us. We need to truly realize that all our power is in Christ. If we do, then we will operate just fine. However, if we keep thinking the power is a mixture of our resolve plus God's response, then we will only function on a limited basis at best.

I want to share with you what the word, strong, means in this verse. The Greek word is ĕndunamŏō which means, to empower. It comes from two words. The first is ĕn, a prime particle, and it means, a fixed position. The second word is dunamis which many of you probably recognize as the word which means, the miracle power of God. Put it all together and you'll see Paul is saying to Timothy, "Remain in the position of the miracle power of God. Do this by staying in grace."

Wouldn't you like to be living in God's miracle power? How would you like to be in a fixed position, in other words, knowing God's power is always in you? Well, it's no mystery. I don't care if you've heard twenty thousand messages about attaining the miracle power of God through some self made means. The word here is that by being strong in the grace in Christ Jesus, you will be always in the very place of power.

Again, our natural selves don't like that. We want to make it more difficult. We want to take the credit for assuming God's power in our own lives, and if we are not doing that then we usually make it more difficult by simply refusing to believe it would be that simple. We naturally assume the Christian who gets the miracle power of God working in his life must be the few and far in between cases. He must be the exception to the rule. Actually, nothing could be further from the truth. God wants you to realize the joy of living in His power and, because He loves you, He has made it easily available to you and in you by His grace. But, as so often is the case, the very simplicity of it has become a major stumbling block to many. They are so busy beating their heads against the wall trying to figure it out, that they can't see the answer which is right in front of them.

Grace is my strength. How I praise God for grace. You know, because my strength is in grace, I am able to be strong all the time. Before, when I thought strength was a matter of my obedience and commitment, I would fall down a lot, and I knew how litle strength I had. I still fall down a lot, and I know now I don't have any strength at all when it comes to living in the Sprit of God, and yet I'm stronger than I've ever been! Hallelujah! I now know my strength isn't measured by what I feel. My strength is in God's grace. So, when I feel completely exhausted and without any power at all, I know that doesn't matter. God is in me, and He is in control. He is strong, and He is my strength.

What a beautiful release! What a joy to know I am strong because He is my strength. I am free from fear, because I don't trust in my own abilities or lack of abilities. I don't have to worry about losing anything, because Jesus is my strength. He is greater than I am, and when I take my eyes off myself to look at Him, I am put in touch with His overcoming power. I can now see situations turn around before my very eyes, because I have chosen to be strong in His grace rather than in my own power.

This is true strength; to realize Jesus is everything and all He asks you to do is to trust in His power. A simple faith in God's ability makes all the difference in the world.

If you choose to remain in this awareness of grace, then you will always be standing firm in the Lord and in the power of His might. In his letter to the church at Rome, Paul said, ". . . Through whom (Jesus) also we have obtained our introduction by faith into this grace in which we stand" (5:2). In this letter, perhaps more than any other he wrote, Paul carefully laid out just exactly what he believed. The church at Rome differed from the other churches Paul wrote to in that he had never visited this church. Ephesians, Philippians, Colossians, Thessalonians; all of these were churches Paul had either founded or had a direct involvement through one of his co-workers in founding. But the church at Rome had begun without him. For many years he had hoped to see this congregation and now he thought at last that the time was drawing near when he would finally have this long standing desire of his fulfilled. He sent off this lengthly epistle to greet his brethren in Rome and also to acquaint them with the Gospel he preached. For this reason, Romans is a very significant letter and probably Paul's most carefully constructed one as well.

So, with this understanding, we see how important a phrase is written here concerning the grace in which we stand. Paul is saying throughout this letter that grace is the ground we stand upon in victory as believers.

Notice, we stand in grace. We don't attempt to attain to grace, we are already standing in it. We don't fight for it, we already have it.

To stand somewhere means you recognize where you are and that's all you do. Abide is another suitable word for stand and, in fact, the Greek bears this out in this particular verse. Once you realize grace is your strength, you will most certainly stand in it. If you are to be Christ-centered then to stand in grace is to stand in the direct center. Everything else will have a perfect flow and continuity to it as you stand in the center.

As he closed his first letter, Peter concluded by saying, "I have written to you briefly, exhorting and testifying that this is the true grace of God. Stand firm in it!" (1st Peter 5:12). You can't find any stronger wording anywhere else in the Bible concerning our lives in Christ. Stand firm in the grace of God. This is not a suggestion, it's a command. It's not an option, it's the only way.

Are you ready to stand firm in the grace of God? Are you convinced there is no other place to be? Are you sure your strength is in grace? It's your choice. You can go on chasing every wind of doctrine hoping to find some short-cut to spirituality that will let you share in the credit, or you can give up and give in to the all encompassing grace of God. You can continue in varied and strange teachings, or you can let grace be sufficient for you.

Grace is the only place to be. In my day of trial, I know if I'm standing in anything other than grace, I'll be sure to fall. But, if grace is my strength and if I'm standing firm in it, I know I *will* stand no matter how great a flood beats against my house. Grace is the center of the Gospel and that's why God's power is in grace. Remember, grace is the true nature and essence of our Lord Jesus Christ, so to stand in grace is to stand in Jesus, allowing our full trust to be in Him, and in Him alone.

Today, if you will hear his voice, harden not your heart. Stop playing the games of a "me plus God" Christianity and stop putting up with those who try to sway you into their own self-conceived brand of spirituality. There is no real truth in those things.

They are like the Emperor's new clothes. The emperor, as the story goes, was wearing nothing, but nobody would say so because they were afraid everybody else would think them to be stupid. A lot of "pop-theology" is just like that. People are afraid to question it for fear of their peers thinking them to be spiritually inferior, so they remain silent, and the emperor parades about wearing absolutely nothing at all. Many of these so-called "deeper life teachings" place a high premium upon what their proponents call "Knowing". This knowing is nothing more than a clever disguise because the fact is, their dogmatic teachings make no sense when you look at the Bible in context. If you question them you're made to feel you must be too stupid to realize what they are talking about, so you wind up just taking their word for it. But, if you are willing to take a close look at the Scriptures which they carefully weave together, often at the expense of context and what the rest of the Bible has to say, you will see their concepts to be nothing more than a house of cards, ready to fall at the slightest inquiry.

True Christianity is Jesus Christ. He's the beginning, the middle, and the end. All we are are recipients of God's grace. We are products of what His grace accomplishes. Our yieldedness to His will is all He asks, and that is so He can have the opportunity to make us a new creation and then transform us from glory to glory as we grow in Him.

Any theology which places the burden upon you is a mistaken belief. Jesus secured your salvation; you just accept what He has done. God causes your growth; you yield yourself to His will. Grace produces your obedience, your fruit, your hope, your fullness, your freedom from sin, and your strength. You simply respond to what God has done.

This is the true grace of God. Stand firm in it. Let God be God. In other words, let Him be as big as He really is. You know, every time you attempt to bring about blessing by your own power, you are only making God smaller. He is big. He is bigger than you or I will ever know. If you will let your strength be in His grace, and if you will stand in grace, then you will be giving God the opportunity to reveal Himself to you in His bigness.

This is what He desires each of His children to know. He waits for us to trust fully in Him. His desire is to show us how strong He is. Our own efforts only hinder His power in our lives.

Choose. Continue in the games, or let God have full control. The decision you make will determine whether you follow after Jesus, or follow after man's restructuring of Jesus. Jesus said to His true disciples, "Come, follow Me." I trust you will make the right choice.

# Chapter 25

# A Warning From God

*"I do not nullify the grace of God; for if righteousness comes through the law, then Christ died needlessly."*

*Galatians 2:21*


*"You have been severed from Christ, you who are seeking to be justified by law; you have fallen from grace."*

*Galatians 5:4*


*"See to it that no one comes short of the grace of God; that no root of bitterness springing up causes trouble, and by it many be defiled."*

*Hebrews 12:15*


There is a danger! The Bible says, "To whom much is given, much is required" (Luke 12:48). The person who has had the Gospel of salvation in Jesus Christ presented to him and then rejects that Gospel will come to a day of judgment where he will have to pay the penalty for his decision. He may try to explain his way out of the situation by saying he never *really* rejected Christ, but the fact that he never really accepted Christ as Savior will be the deciding issue. "To whom much is given, much is required." When you are given the good news of the Gospel, you are placed in the position of having to make a choice. You either choose Christ, or you reject Him. To make no decision is the same as rejecting Him. At the end of this age, multitudes will be cast into the lake of fire, where they will undergo eternal torment. It's a hideous and heart-sickening thought, but we need to see that every soul who makes that fatal descent into the place prepared for the devil, will have gone there on his own free will. God does not assign anyone to the lake of fire. Every single person who is cast into that horrible fate will know there was a time when he or she had the opportunity to choose Jesus Christ and they let it pass. For them the phrase, "To whom much is given, much is required" will be all too unfortunately real.

So it is with us. We, who have chosen the Lord, are also facing a decision. Our decision is not whether we will receive or reject Jesus as Savior. We have accepted Him and we have been gloriously born anew into the kingdom of God. That's not the choice I'm speaking of. I mean we have to now choose or reject Jesus as our *ongoing* life.

I have presented you with the grace of God. Hopefully you have joyously responded to the things I have shared with you in this book. I trust your eyes have opened to a whole new way of peace, joy, and utter fulfillment in God. However, I would be remiss if I did not tell you what God's word says to those who, as believers, choose to neglect the grace of God. Grace is God's ultimate revelation of Himself. When we are confronted with grace, we must respond. We either yield the leadership of our Christian experience to Him, and to His grace. or we simply pay lip service to grace and continue on after our own inventions of spiritual living. We either allow Jesus to be our absolute fullness in every way, or we ignore His grace and opt for the more naturally satisfying avenues of self-made Christianity. "To whom much is given, much is required."

I trust by now you realize how important grace is and how central it is concerning everything in Jesus. Just review the chapter titles we have already covered and you will see that grace is indeed the heart of our faith. But, as is the case concerning salvation, God's word has a strong exhortation to His children about the grace He has so freely given.

Paul wrote his letter to the Galatian churches in response to those who were claiming grace was only significant for salvation and that the law needed to be adhered to if you wanted to "stay saved." We have already discussed this in earlier chapters. What I would like to share with you now from Galatians is what Paul had to say regarding those who thought their righteousness came from their efforts; in this case, from their obedience to the law. Remember, the law basically says, "Do this and you will be blessed." You earn the blessing under the system of law. Grace says, "I've done it all and I give it all to you as a gift." You cannot earn the blessing in grace because Jesus Christ has done it all. Moreover, you couldn't earn the blessing no matter how hard you tried. This is why following after the law is living a lie. Jesus fulfilled the law at Calvary and He offers us the blessing of being in His presence apart from our futile efforts at trying to fulfill the law ourselves. We are released from the burden of trying to win and keep our salvation. That is grace.

In Paul's impassioned discourse in chapter two of Galatians, he wrote, "I do not nullify the grace of God; for if righteousness comes through the law, then Christ died needlessly" (2:21). Paul was saying that living in any system which attempts to gain righteousness by our own efforts would be tantamount to nullifying God's grace. Not only that, but Paul went on to state that we would be saying Jesus died needlessly. His death wasn't necessary. There is no greater insult a Christian could possibly give to his God than to tell Him Jesus' death wasn't really necessary.

Now, you may indeed be living according to some external code of conduct which you believe gives you your growth and blessing in Christ, and you may say to me that you don't feel Jesus died needlessly. You may say you praise Him every day for your salvation. But the point here is that it doesn't matter what you say or think. The plain truth is, if you're living under the illusion that being a Christian revolves around obeying the law then, as far as God is concerned, you are telling Him you don't think His death for you was all that important. Your life says what you believe. If you live in anything other than grace, you are casting off Jesus.

Don't believe the lie that grace is only for salvation, and that works and obedience determine whether you remain a child of God or not. This is the same thing the Galatian Christians were told. The tune may vary from church to church, but the thrust of the message remains the same.

Jesus died to pay for your sins, and in His death and resurrection is salvation. But man has redefined salvation to mean "accepting Jesus and being born again." In other words, man has changed the meaning of salvation so that it is only relevant to your initial experience with Christ. But God's word defines salvation as all encompassing. A beginning to end salvation is what Jesus died for. So, those who institute some "works plus God" method of growth after being born again are simply throwing God's salvation back in His face. It's as if they are saying, "Thanks for the boost God, now we'll take it from here." God has always intended the salvation He purchased with His own blood to be understood as a complete, every moment of your life, salvation. The grace which brought you into Jesus in the first place has always been intended to keep you in Jesus and bring you finally, at the last day, into the complete presence of God. This is God's definition of salvation; not some momentary blissful connection with Christ, but your entire life in Christ as well! To live with any other understanding is to nullify the grace of God and proclaim by your actions that you believe Christ died needlessly.

The Greek word for nullify in this verse is athĕtĕō which means; to set aside, neutralize, cast off, and reject. As soon as you take your eyes off of Jesus, no matter how convincing the argument is, you automatically neutralize God's grace in your life. It's as we saw in Romans chapter eleven. Grace and works can not be mixed, otherwise grace is no longer grace. Grace can't be mixed with anything. It can't be mixed with the law. It can't be mixed with your efforts. Grace must stand alone. You must understand at all times that everything you have is because of grace, and everything you need is found in grace. Anything else is a rejection of God's grace.

Later on, in chapter five of this letter Paul said, "You have been severed from Christ, you who are seeking to be justified by law; you have fallen from grace" (verse 4). You know I've actually heard messages by people who preach the law on this verse. They completely rip this Scripture out of context and deliver some hard-hitting message on sin. They say when you sin you fall from grace, so make sure you never sin. From there they go into their own special prescription of God's laws and their own pet rules. They would have you believe that by strict adherence to their teaching, you will at last arrive at the place of sinless perfection. So they set aside grace, and from the way they misuse this verse, it's clear they never understood grace in the first place. Actually this verse in context, is an indictment against these very people.

Let's back up a bit and catch the flow of what Paul was saying. "It was for freedom that Christ set us free; therefore keep standing firm and do not be subject again to a yoke of slavery. Behold I, Paul, say to you that if you receive circumcision, Christ will be of no benefit to you. And I testify again to every man who receives circumcision, that he is under obligation to keep the whole law. You have been severed from Christ, you who are seeking to be justified by law; you have fallen from grace" (5:1-4).

Who fell from grace? Was it some poor soul who fell into sin? No, it was the one who tried to achieve righteousness through the law. This is the one who has been severed from Christ.

There is something very significant here. Notice in verse 3 Paul declares that if you just try to obey one of the laws, you are therefore required to obey them all. In other words, you would have to try to earn your salvation by the law. These so called "Judaisers" were very clever, but they were also very wrong. They thought they could convince the new Galatian Christians to see that Jesus saved them to only make them obey the law. However, Paul clearly explained here that there is no such thing as a little law and a little grace. There is only all law, or all grace. To say you are saved by grace, and to believe there are laws you must adhere to in order to keep saved, or in order to promote growth, is to really throw God's grace completely away. You simply reject salvation and place yourself in the position of having to earn everything. Now, you may not believe that, but the point is, this is what the Bible says. You either have to accept what Scripture says, or you will go off after your own created brand of Christianity.

Again, in these verses, we see Paul saying that to reject grace is to reject Christ. Our justification, our righteousness, indeed our everything is through grace and not through the system of law. There will probably always be those who preach a homogenization of grace and law instead of the Biblically accurate truth of grace fulfilling the law. They will continue to say the law is our boundary, as if grace isn't enough. They will continue to make you feel that you prove your dedication to God by how hard you work and how well you obey their laws. They will always be putting the cart before the horse. Obedience will earn grace and blessing in their eyes. They won't see that grace produces obedience. They won't see grace motivates us to love and good deeds, and does it with joy and blessing. They will never stop long enough to ask the simple question, "Where is the law today?" They will just keep on assuming that the law is at least as relevant to us today as is grace. The sad thing is, they will feel as if they are proclaiming Christ, when in fact God's word says their theology is actually severed from Christ and is making His finished work of none effect in the lives of those who listen to their messages.

The writer of Hebrews put it this way. He said, "See to it that no one comes short of the grace of God; that no root of bitterness springing up causes trouble, and by it many be defiled" (12:15). God has certainly shown me the reality of this verse. I have seen Christians react angrily and violently to the message of grace. I've beheld ministers who almost foam at the mouth and gnash their teeth when the grace of God is lifted up in Spirit and in truth.

Grace touches a tender nerve within them. The root of course, is the refusal to believe God could be so big and loving. They define God according to their standards. If they expect people to pay for wrong doing, then they assume God expects His children to pay for wrong doing. They don't let God lift them up to His level. They instead drag Him down to their level.

To them, the message of grace is "soft-soap Christianity." It's repulsive to them, because they have no depth of understanding concerning the true ministry and purpose of Jesus Christ. They have stopped short of grace, and bitterness is the result.

If you don't live in grace, you will find yourself measuring the spirituality of your brothers and sisters according to whatever laws you ascribe to. You will find yourself disdainful of those who have different beliefs from yours. You will be completely outside of the heart of God and living instead in a box of rules and regulations.

The writer of Hebrews goes on, and what he next says truly reveals the impact of what a Christian actually does when he lives outside of grace. This is a hard word, but it is the truth. He said, "That there be no immoral person like Esau, who sold his own birthright for a single meal" (verse 16).

As far as God is concerned, when one of His children comes short of grace, he is in reality selling his birthright. Do you see that? Now do you understand the importance of grace in your own life? Do you see the responsibility you have to live before the Lord, all the days of your life, in His grace?

Esau was Isaac's first born but he regarded that blessing lightly. One day, he came in from hunting and he was hungry. Jacob was cooking a stew, and in his hunger, Esau felt his appetite was more important than his own birthright so he sold it to Jacob for a bowl of stew. Esau's main mistake was that he valued something more than his birthright.

You and I have been given a birthright; grace. We must never let anything become more important to us than our birthright. We must stay in grace, in Christ. Every day we must live in the grace of God. We can't allow anything or anyone to try and convince us away from God's grace. If we do, then we will be selling our birthright. We will be falling from grace. We will be making God's grace of none effect in our lives. We will be experientially severing ourselves from Christ and saying with our actions that we believe our Lord died needlessly. To live in anything other than a 100% grace relationship is to do all of these things.

So, as I said, there is a danger. The danger is that you could take everything I've shared with you and then just assign it to some corner of your Christianity. If you do that, you will be actually throwing away all I've shared with you. You will be nullifying grace. You will be falling from grace. You will be coming short of grace.

You have heard the word of grace, and now you are responsible before God, just like the unbeliever who hears the Gospel. You must make a decision, and as I said, to make no decision is really a rejection of the message. It is of primary importance to our Lord that you choose to live totally in His grace.

Yes, there is a responsibility on your part, but it is really a most blessed responsibility. God has opened the doors of abundant life to you and now He asks you to choose. Come all the way into Him in His fullness or, continue trying to achieve this free gift through your own efforts. I trust your decision will not be a hard one to make.

# Chapter 26

# Let Your Speech Always Be Grace

*"Let your speech always be with grace, seasoned, as it were, with salt, so that you may know how you should respond to each person."*                    *Colossians 4:6*

It is not enough to be only living in grace. We need to speak the word of grace to those around us. The Gospel of God's grace needs to be communicated to the world, and especially to our own brothers and sisters in Christ.

In the fourth chapter of Paul's letter to the Colossian church, he asks for prayer concerning his outreach and message. Beginning in verse 3 he says, "Praying at the same time for us as well, that God may open up to us a door for the Word, so that we may speak forth the mystery of Christ, for which I have also been imprisoned." Paul had wisdom enough to know that before you go presenting the Gospel, you must first have an open door, so this is how he began his prayer request.

Have you ever had the experience of pushing the Gospel into

a conversation, only to later feel reproved by the Spirit of God for doing so? Sometimes we can get so worked up about the need for a person to be saved that we stop looking at the person altogether and we just treat him as some unfeeling statistic. The result of such an approach is that we can actually turn someone off to the Gospel instead of drawing them to the Lord. Don't be so naive as to think if anyone rejects your message, then that must mean they have rejected the Lord. I have frankly heard many a presentation of Christ that has turned me off, and I love the Lord. Sometimes it's not the Lord a person is refusing, rather it's our arrogant and insensitive attitudes they are put off by.

We need to know that how we say something is equally important as what it is we're saying. I'm afraid a Christian can be guilty of thinking because he is sharing the Gospel, it doesn't matter what he says as long as he says it. If this is your attitude, then how can you expect someone to believe in the loving and caring God you're trying to tell them about, when you are being so unloving and so uncaring? How do you expect someone to accept the Prince of Peace into their lives when you are being abrasive and insensitive? You see, the Spirit of the Lord is just as important as the word of the Lord is.

Paul understood this. When he requested this prayer of the Colossians he had already been ministering the Gospel for years. It is not as if he was some nervous rookie going street witnessing for the first time. No, Paul had learned through experience that an open door is imperitive to a fruitful presentation of the Gospel.

He continued in verse 4 by saying, ". . . in order that I might make it clear in the way I ought to speak." Now here is truly a heart which is broken and open to the Lord. Not only did Paul realize he needed an open door before he could speak, but he also knew he needed wisdom from God as to how he ought to speak once the door was open. His desire was that the Gospel be clearly presented, and he knew one person's needs differed from another person's needs so a pat technique of preaching the Gospel just would not do.

How I cringe when I come across some book which pretends to be an authoritative manual on how to preach the Gospel and win souls to Christ. Invariably, the message of Jesus Christ is brought down to the same level as a vacuum cleaner presentation.

You have to make up your mind; are you going after statistics and numbers or are you interested in meeting an individual's deepest needs? Are you out to merely "win a soul" or do you truly care about being a manifestation of Jesus Christ to each person you come in contact with? Do you want to learn a basic guideline or would you rather learn to listen to God's voice in each situation?

Paul had ministered in synagogues, in public speaking places, to Jews, to Greeks, to the poor, to the rich, to the wise of this age, and to the simple. As he grew in the knowledge of Christ he understood one man's need may not be another's, and so he learned to be sensitive to each individual he came in contact with. He echoed this feeling in the next verse when he said, "Conduct yourself with wisdom toward outsiders, making the most of the opportunity" (verse 5).

Yes, we need to make the most of every opportunity we are given, but we also need wisdom so we can tell the difference between what is a real opportunity from God and what we are trying to force upon a person by assuming it to be an opportunity. For instance, the Bible tells us to, "Rejoice with those who rejoice, and weep with those who weep" (Romans 12·15). How many of you realize what a great mistake and injury it would be if you rejoiced with those who weep? Unfortunately, I've seen this happen.

Some believer adopts the praise-God-all-the-time-for-every-thing attitude and he then encounters someone who has just undergone a deep tragedy. The believer, unfortunately, doesn't care about the person's grief; all he cares about is his great one-answer-fits-all doctrine, so he comes down on that individual for being sad. He tells him he needs to stop feeling sorry for himself and he should start praising God in this thing. Has he ministered life? Not necessarily. I'll be the first to admit the power of praise can really turn things around for us, but do you see how this relates to the topic of wisdom? Maybe what that person needed was for a loving brother in Christ to put his arm around him and cry with him. Maybe he needed someone to tell him God really loves him and sees his grief, and is hurt by his pain. Sometimes the last thing a person needs is for some insensitive self professed know it all to come on the scene with his band-aid theology. We need to rejoice with those who rejoice, and we also need to weep with those who weep. The only way we will ever know how to react in the Spirit of God to a situation will be if we lean moment by moment upon the Lord for His wisdom.

So, we need opportunities and open doors. We need to make the most of our opportunities and we need the wisdom to make the message clear. We also need sensitivity to God's Spirit and to the spirit of the person with whom we will be speaking.

Paul concludes this section by saying, "Let your speech always be with grace, seasoned, as it were, with salt, so that you may know how you should respond to each person" (verse 6). The first line literally reads this way: "Your word always in grace" or "Let your speech always be grace." In other words, when you have received the open door, the opportunity, the clear message, and the wisdom, then you can speak, but always speak grace. Grace is the message which will meet every need at its deepest level.

It's like what Jesus said, "If I be lifted up from the earth, (I) will draw all men to Myself" (John 12:32). Grace always lifts up Jesus. Grace is Christ-centered because grace is Jesus, and when Jesus is lifted up, *all* men are drawn to Him. A person who speaks the true word of grace will always be sensitive to an individual's needs, because speaking grace means you yourself will be sensitive to God's heart, therefore you are in a place to have the Spirit of the Lord communicate the proper word and feeling through you to that person's need.

I like the way Paul uses the allegory of our speaking being like seasoning with salt. We put salt on food to bring out the flavor, to enhance the taste. If you were in some fancy restaurant and ordered a twenty dollar steak, what would you do if the waiter came to your table and dumped a whole shaker full of salt on your dish? Would you thank him for enhancing the flavor? No. Most likely you would yell at him and tell him he ruined your beautiful meal.

We should keep this in mind as we speak of Christ. He is our Pearl of Great Price. The Bible says, "Taste and see that the Lord is good" (Psalm 34:8).

If you are insensitive in your presentation of the Gospel, you will be just like the waiter pouring salt all over the steak. You won't help the Lord in this case. You will actually be ruining the message.

I don't know about you, but a steak that is lightly salted tastes just fine to me. I think I would gag on one that had a pound of salt on it. I just would not be able to eat it. It's not that I'd be rejecting the steak. I would probably be eagerly anticipating such a marvelous meal. It's just that the way it was served would make it inedible.

Could it be possible that you have felt someone rejected Christ, when the real truth is that you gave the person you spoke to lousy service? Maybe you machine-gunned someone with 30 Scriptures in a 5 minute period and then wouldn't leave them alone until they made a decision. Maybe you decided that "today was the day of their salvation", when in fact God intended to use a more gradual approach in their lives.

If you will be willing to lay aside your own opinions and compulsions, and instead live in the grace of God, you will be a far more effective servant of the Lord. The word of grace is always a timely word. If you let your speech always be grace, then you will discover the blessing of being able to communicate with someone at their deepest level of need. You will know the joy of being a manifestation of Christ to an individual, and most importantly, you will be walking in, and a true minister of, the Spirit of the living God. The same grace which is ready and willing to transform your life will also be able to transform the lives of those around you if you will simply, "Let your speech always be grace."

# Chapter 27

# Giving Grace

*"Let no unwholesome word proceed from your mouth, but only such a word as is good for edification according to the need of the moment, that it may give grace to those who hear."*

*Ephesians 4:29*

*"But I do not consider my life of any account as dear to myself, in order that I may finish my course, and the ministry I received from the Lord Jesus, to testify solemnly of the Gospel of the grace of God."*

*Acts 20:24*

Once you have become the recipient of grace, you will sense the need to be a communicator of grace to the world around you. In the last chapter we saw that our speech must always be grace. We need to carry in our every thought the knowledge that grace is what needs to be coming from our lips. Grace and truth are realized in Jesus Christ. This is the message of John 1:17. Hopefully our desire for everyone we come in contact with will be for them to see a realization of Jesus in our lives and speech. They will be able to if we hold up grace and truth.

Our thoughts and words have to come under the scrutiny of the Holy Spirit. How casually and carelessly some allow their words to be. To many the saying, "Look before you leap" seems to be the antithesis of the way their words are chosen. "Speaking off the top of their heads" is an unfortunately more accurate description of so many, and tragically this same attitude is rampant in the body of Christ.

Our words are a ministry. If we act as though our words exist only to verbalize our feelings, then I'm afraid we will do much damage to those around us. Particularly for us as Christians, every word which proceeds out of our mouths will either minister death or life to the hearer. I'm not saying we can't ever express our own needs and sentiments, but I am saying we need to have a larger field of vision concerning our needs.

Proverbs 12:18 says, "There is one who speaks rashly like the thrusts of a sword, but the tongue of the wise brings healing." Which of these qualities do you find yourself identifying with most often? Are you a healer or a sword-thruster? The phrase, "Speaks rashly" comes from one Hebrew word, bâtâ, and it means to babble, to voice angrily, and to speak unadvisedly. Do you find your passion and emotion overcoming the Spirit of wisdom and compassion? If you do, then you need to have the Lord touch you in this area.

James tells us in his letter that no man can tame the tongue. Unfortunately, we will always be making mistakes in what we say and when we speak. But the Bible certainly does not advocate an "I don't care" attitude either. We need to recognize the crucial importance our words play in the lives of those around us, and we need to lean completely upon the Lord regarding our tongues.

The tongue of the wise brings healing. This is our goal. As we learn to speak in grace, we will see healing take place. Grace can remove mountains, and sometimes the greatest mountains facing us are the feelings, attitudes, and problems in the lives of those we live near. A word of grace, rightly chosen, can melt away hardness and bitterness. Grace can change lives. It has changed ours and we can see it change others if we will diligently seek to be ministers of grace.

Again in the book of Proverbs we find this word of wisdom, "A gentle answer turns away wrath, but a harsh word stirs up anger" (15:1). We must learn to live beyond the narrow and confining scope of our own opinions. We need to see our tongue as a vessel of life or death. A soft and gentle word can diffuse a volatile situation, but if we project our criticism and judgment, then our harsh words will only bring death into the atmosphere. God has given us the ability to speak, not so we can merely say what we think, but so we can "proclaim the excellencies of Him who called us out of darkness into His marvelous light" (1st Peter 2:9). We need to understand it is of equal importance that we be communicators of grace, just as we need to be constant recipients of grace.

In the practical section of his letter to the Ephesian church, Paul had this to say, "Let no unwholesome word proceed from your mouth, but only such a word as is good for edification according to the need of the moment, that it may give grace to those who hear" (4:29). Here is the true Christian attitude toward our words. We should have it fixed in our hearts that we will only encourage and give the proper word at the proper time so that those who hear might receive grace from us. The Greek word for unwholesome in this verse means to be rotten and worthless. We truly need to understand that any word coming out of our mouth which is not grace and does not encourage the hearers is a rotten and worthless word. I'm sure the reason why so many believers fail to see this is because they actually feel their opinions and observations are valid, worthy, and must be in agreement with God's mind. This is one of the main hold-overs from our lives before we knew Christ. All that mattered then was what we thought. We were the center of our lives and so we naturally assumed every thought we had was right and every thought someone opposing had must be wrong. All that mattered to us was *us,* and we just didn't have time to truly see another's heart.

How sad it is that this major area of our lives goes completely unchecked by so many believers. If I could pin-point one thing which renders many a Christian ineffective in proclaiming the Gospel, this would be it. Our words are merely manifestations of where our hearts are. If our hearts are tuned to the Lord, then our words will be likewise. But if underneath all the pretenses our hearts are still operating on the same basis, and according to the same principles that they always have, then our words will manifest that. Christianity was never meant to be some sort of a spiritual face lift. Christianity has always been meant to utterly transform us from the old self we've been all our lives into a completely new creation in Jesus Christ.

One very significant step you can take in seeing this transformation occur in your own life is by yielding your heart and tongue to the Lord's grace. If you will agree with what God's word says concerning this, and if you will walk in a moment-by-moment consciousness concerning the necessity of having each word chosen of God, then you will truly begin to see change take place. Ask God to give you His heart attitude towards those around you, and you will discover grace and edification coming forth from your innermost being.

In an earlier chapter, we looked at Paul's farewell address to the Ephesian elders as it is recorded in the twentieth chapter of the book of Acts. I'd like to return to this and share with you what Paul felt about being a communicator of grace. In verse 24 he said, "But I do not consider my life of any account as dear to myself, in order that I may finish my course, and the ministry I received from the Lord Jesus, to testify solemnly of the Gospel of the grace of God."

What was the ministry Paul received from the Lord? It was to testify solemnly of the Gospel of the grace of God. We can read through Acts, through all of Paul's epistles, and we can see all the issues he wrote about and all the experiences he went through. But in his own words, we see him summing up everything by saying he was called of the Lord to testify solemnly of the Gospel of the grace of God. In other words, if everything else was taken away and only one thing left, that one thing would be to testify solemnly of the Gospel of the grace of God.

This divine mission from God was even more important to Paul than his own life. You see, Paul had been touched by grace. He confessed that the sufferings of this life couldn't be compared to the glories of the next (2nd Corinthians 4:17&18). He knew when he was weak he was strong (2nd Corinthians 12:10). He knew God would forever meet all of his needs in Christ regardless of whether he was in affliction or prosperity (Philippians 4:11-14). When he said he didn't consider his life as being of any account to himself, he wasn't saying he didn't care about life. He wasn't consigning himself to misery as if somehow this was God's will for him. No, what he was saying was that God's grace was more important to him than his own life. He knew he could receive more in a moment of grace than he could in a lifetime of whatever the world could offer him.

Paul's supreme reason for existence was to be a recipient of grace, and he recognized his supreme reason for remaining in this three dimensional world was to be a communicator of that same grace. Even if everything he held dear in this life was to be lost, as indeed it was, that simply would not matter because he had received grace and was commissioned by God to reveal grace to the world he lived in.

Paul was a man who was touched by God at the very deepest level. His tongue could not help but speak of grace because his heart and mind had been completely transformed. Although Paul was bodily alive in a time and space existence, he was truly living in a different world, in a world called the kingdom of God. Everything he came in contact with was seen through different eyes than the eyes of natural man, because Paul had been conquered by God's grace and could never again be the same. He once said, "Woe is me if I do not preach the Gospel" (1st Corinthians 9:16). He had no choice. There was only one thing in his heart and that was to minister the Lord Jesus Christ in all of His grace and truth. The work of grace was complete in the life of Paul and so, for him, there was simply nothing else to speak of than God's grace.

May we seek this same depth-unto-depth transformation. May we realize the utter worthlessness of our own words, values, and opinions. May we fall upon the Lord in despair of our own natural condition and may we be changed into continual recipients and communicators of the grace of God. When this becomes our heart's desire, then we truly will be giving grace to

**those who hear.**

# Chapter 28

# Grace Reigns

*"Even so grace might reign through righteousness to eternal life through Jesus Christ our Lord."*                    **Romans 5:21**

*"For if by the transgression of the one, death reigned through the one, much more those who receive the abundance of grace and of the gift of righteousness will reign in life through the one, Jesus Christ."*                    **Romans 5:17**

Grace is stronger than sin! There could be no better current news for the Christian than this glorious truth. No matter how great a particular sin may be in our lives, the good news is that we are no longer enslaved to that sin because God has given us grace and His grace is stronger than any sin.

Back in chapter six, we saw how grace has given us freedom from sin. The basic principle at work is the fact that grace is stronger than sin. If you go to a church where the preacher assumes that speaking about the dangers of sin will give you the inner resolve to resist sin, most likely you won't find any real help there. You may in fact discover sin has a greater hold upon you than it ever had. The reason for this is because looking at sin won't free you from its power. Preaching against sin won't free you from sin either. There is only one thing which brings a true and lasting victory over sin, and that is grace. Telling a Christian he shouldn't sin is like telling a drowning man he shouldn't go under. Your advice is great, but it's without any power to change things. The only way to solve a problem is to look at the solution, and grace is the solution to any problem in our lives.

Because grace is in Jesus, and is the true nature of Jesus, we can see the victory which it has won. Grace is victorious over sin, death, and the law. Grace has hurdled every barrier and has crossed the finish line on your behalf. Romans chapter five says, "And the law came in that the transgression might increase; but where sin increased, grace abounded all the more, that, as sin reigned in death, even so grace might reign through righteousness to eternal life through Jesus Christ our Lord" (verses 20&21). A number of significant things are stated here. First, there is the startling remark that the law came in so that sin might increase! This may sound incredible at first, and the only way it will ever make any sense will be if you understand the purpose of the law. The law was not given, as so many suggest, to point us to God. Instead the opposite is true. The law was given to show us our sin. Why would God institute a system of His ordinances which could only make us aware of our failures? The answer is very simple. God knows no one can come to Him on their own strength. But the problem is we don't know that, so He gave us the law to show us our complete inability to approach Him. The law came in so that our sin would be even more apparent to us, hopefully with the result that we would realize our need for a Savior. As Galatians 3:24

says, "The law has become our tutor to lead us to Christ, that we may be justified by faith." This is why 1st Corinthians makes the remark that, "The power of sin is the law" (15:56). The law simply made us more acutely aware of sin, thus sin's power was increased in our lives. As Romans 3:20 tells us, "Through the law comes the knowledge of sin." I have gone over all this ground to once again remind you that the law will never give you victory, as some ministers would have you believe. The law has, from its very inception, had only one purpose and that purpose was to defeat you. So, even as a Christian who has tasted the power of God in Jesus Christ, don't be misled into some strange spiritual brew of grace and the law. The law was given so that the transgression might increase, and so that you might call upon the grace of the Lord to save you and keep you.

The next thing we are told from this passasge is that where sin increased grace abounded all the more. This may seem hard to understand at first. We need to back up to verse 15 where we are told, "For if by the transgression of the one the many died (referring to Adam's sin and how it infected all mankind), much more did the grace of God and the gift by the grace of the one man, Jesus Christ, abound to the many." You see, sin came into the picture when Adam rejected God's word about the tree of the knowledge of good and evil. The Lord had specifically told Adam not to eat from this tree, but he went ahead and ate from it anyway. At that moment he fell and developed an independent personality. This independence from God was known as sin. Adam failed and sin was the consequence. But another man came on the scene, Jesus Christ, and He did not fail. He lived His life in complete accord with His heavenly Father and grace was the result of His obedience to God's will. Adam failed and gave us sin. Jesus was victorious and gave us grace, therefore grace is stronger than sin. Sin was the product of Adam's weakness. Grace was the product of Jesus' strength.

Where sin increased, grace abounded all the more. No matter how many sins man committed, the day was coming when Jesus would willingly lay down His life at Calvary to pay for all the sins of the world. So, no matter how sin increased, grace was ultimately greater. Jesus' victory on our behalf was greater than Adam's failure. The fact that you and I are born again is testimony of this truth. Sin could not hold us in its grasp. We were freed the moment we received Jesus Christ as our own Lord and Savior.

Verse 21 goes on to say, "sin reigned in death." This was the final manifestation of sin. Death came, the eternal separation from God, as sin had its final course in man's life. Thankfully for us, the verse goes on to say, "even so grace might reign through righteousness to eternal life through Jesus Christ our Lord." Sin's victory was manifest in death, but our great Lord Jesus has made grace manifest its victory in life! The fabulous news declared in this verse for all believers is that, "grace might reign through righteousness to eternal life." In other words, grace will keep on reigning in our lives from the moment we receive Christ right up to the moment we finally see Him face to face. There will be no break in the victory grace has won for us. We can rest, assured that "He who began a good work in you will perfect it unto the day of Christ Jesus" (Philippians 1:6). And, as verse 21 tells us, this victory is maintained "through Jesus Christ our Lord."

Grace is victorious. There is no power in the whole universe which can come near to the power of God's grace. All of eternity will simply be a testimony of the fact that grace is reigning in life.

Many an earth born ruler has come and gone who wished he could establish an eternal reign for his family. But Jesus Christ has won the victory through His grace and His triumph will last forever and ever. There will simply be no end to the reign of grace, and this is why we have the word eternity given to us. Eternity describes the reign of God's grace.

Yes, grace reigns, but the Bible also says we reign because of God's grace. It's important to recognize the victory of grace, but it is equally important for you to become personally identified with this victory. You reign! Romans 5:17 declares, "For if by the transgression of the one, death reigned through the one (Adam), much more those who receive the abundance of grace (that's you) and of the gift of righteousness will reign in life through the One, Jesus Christ."

The victory of grace is not just for some future eternity, it is for right now too. It is more accurate to say that eternity begins for you the moment you receive Christ into your life.

Grace reigns. Grace is the supreme power over all of God's creation. Turn to this victory in your own life and let it become effective in you. When sin, or the law, comes knocking at your door trying to bring you down, turn to grace and let the victory of Jesus Christ be your victory too. Fix your eyes upon Jesus, and let the knowledge of your reigning in life become reality to you.

Sometimes we get so used to our shortcomings that we all but forget that our salvation is a victorious salvation. It seems we so easily let our eyes get taken off what Christ has accomplished and instead of feasting upon His goodness, power, and ability to work all things for good in our lives, all we see is our sins and problems. Remember, the Scripture says where sin increased grace abounded all the more.

Instead of seeing the increase of sin in your life, I encourage you to look at the abounding of grace in you. The Bible says you are to reign in life, and that means right now. Don't wait for heaven to arrive before you start to enjoy your victory. Receive it now. Let God place you above your enemies. Let Him seat you in heavenly places in Him. Let the victory of grace take control of your life and watch your outlook change as you become identified with what Christ has done.

Verse 21 says, "grace reigns through righteousness." This is the practical application part of this Scripture. 1st Corinthians 1:30 says Jesus is our righteousness, and Romans 5:19 declares we have been made righteous. It is no boast or bragging for a Christian to say he is righteous. This is what Scriptures says. So, if the Bible says grace reigns through righteousness, then that means we must look to our righteousness in order to see grace reigning. To see yourself as righteous is to look at your new creation. It's to see yourself the way God sees you every moment of every day. If you will choose to see yourself in Christ today, in your righteousness, then I can guarantee you that you will be experiencing the reigning power of grace in your life.

The truth is, you have been given the greatest victory of all time. You are part of this victory because God has made you a part of it. Show the Lord that you truly appreciate what He has done on your behalf. Live in this victory. Rejoice in it every day. Do this and you will be showing the Lord that you are truly thankful for the great things He has done.

# Chapter 29

# God Bears Witness
# to His Grace

*"Therefore they spent a long time there speaking boldly with reliance upon the Lord, who was bearing witness to the word of His grace, granting that signs and wonders be done by their hands."*

*Acts 14:3*

*"And Stephen, full of grace and power, was performing great wonders and signs among the people."*     *Acts 6:8*

I remember a time in my infancy as a Christian when I had an unquenchable desire to see a miraculous manifestation of God. I felt like I really needed to see some great work of God in front of my own eyes. I assumed this would bring about a big increase of my faith. I thought my ministry would have more of a validity to it if the word was out that great things were happening through my hands.

One night I was deep in prayer about this. My mind had been made up and I assumed God was pleased with my desire concerning this. Finally He spoke, and what He laid upon my heart changed me forever. I don't remember the exact words, but the content of the message was this. He said, "Wayne, as long as you seek Me for miracles I will withold them from you. But if you will seek Me and Me only, I will show you more miracles than you could ever dream possible!"

How stupid I had been. I had let myself regard something as more important than the Lord Himself. I had really thought miracles were what I needed, when the truth was I needed to become more dependent upon God. He is the giver of all good things, and yet I had focused my attention upon the gift rather than the Giver.

That was an important crossroads experience for me. I could have gone down the path of always seeking things from God, but how I praise His name that He loved me enough to rebuke me and show me that He is the one I must always seek.

God has proved His word true to me on many occasions concerning His message that night. At that time my ministry consisted pretty much of singing in coffee houses and witnessing on the streets. After doing this for a couple of years, God impressed upon my heart that I needed to lay aside the ministry and just seek Him.

This was a hard word for me because I was used to being a doer. But God had to show me that I still needed to learn the basic lesson. This time the application was that I had to seek Him instead of seeking my ministry. Once again I was taught how easy it is for us to let something become bigger than God, and many times it's the very things we do in God's name which we allow to be more important to us than He is.

I laid aside all I was doing and enrolled in a two year seminary program. Just prior to my going away to school, I attended a crusade being held by Kathryn Kuhlman. During the service, when God's healing power was sweeping across the auditorium and thousands were being touched, Miss Kuhlman paused for a moment. I felt that God was going to say something significant. A strange look came over her and she said, "Right now, at this moment, ask God whatever you want and He will give it to you." I don't know if anyone else in that service heard those words, but I sure knew I did, and I knew this was why God had brought me to that particular crusade. When she uttered those words, my immediate response was, "God, all I want is to serve You and love You all the days of my life. I don't want anything from You, for You are all I want."

I knew God heard me, and I knew He was pleased with my genuine heart felt response. You see, between the time when God first spoke to me that night and the time when I was at the crusade, something very important had happened to me. I had stopped seeking God for signs and wonders, and I had begun seeking Him. I learned what it was to minister to the Lord, and I knew this was why God had created me. He had called me into existence to be a minister unto Him. Our relationship mushroomed and I began to know on a daily basis the incredibly intimate relationship He had called me to. He became my one desire.

And now, ten years later, the words are still true, and even more so. God is my portion. He is my all in all, and I know my primary purpose in this life is to minister unto Him, to praise His name, to live in His presence adoring Him, and to know our oneness of He in me and I in Him. Everything else is secondary to this most holy call.

You may ask, what about the miracles? God has been more than abundant to me. I've seen Him create a ministry in radio, literature, crusades, record albums, and in cassette tapes. I have seen thousands born again into His kingdom. I've seen diseases cured instantaneously in my crusades and also through the radio ministry. I've witnessed His hand in my life turning disaster into victory in a way in which only He could do it.

I can only consider myself blessed. He is the worker of all these things and as long as the eyes of my spirit are kept upon Him living His life in me, I know He will continue to bear witness to His grace through signs and wonders. I can continue to enjoy my simple trusting relationship with Him, and He will continue to bring forth His power in the way He sees fit.

The reason I'm sharing this with you is because I feel it is so important that we never make the mistake of taking our attention off of the Lord to instead let our focus be upon some "thing" we want from Him. I tell you, keep your eyes fixed upon Jesus. Stay in His grace, and God will confirm His word to you time and time again. Walk in faith, trust Him in all things, and don't ever let any need you may have become more important to you than your Lord and Savior Jesus.

We've seen how God's victory is in grace. We have also seen that God's power is in grace. I want to show you now that as you trust completely in His grace, you will be in the very place to realize the miraculous power of God in you and through you.

In the book of Acts, we have this important account given to us, "And it came about that in Iconium they entered the synagogue of the Jews together, and spoke in such a manner that a great multitude believed, both of Jews and of Greeks. But the

Jews who disbelieved stirred up the minds of the gentiles, and embittered them against the brethren. Therefore they spent a long time there speaking boldly with reliance upon the Lord, who was *bearing witness to the word of His grace, granting that signs and wonders be done by their hands"* (14:1-3).

This is so significant. What did Paul and Barnabas do? They preached the grace of God. What did God do? He bore witness to the word of grace by performing signs and wonders through the hands of His disciples. They lifted up Jesus and God testified to the truth of their message. Do you see this? Paul and Barnabas didn't go to Iconium to perform miracles. They went there to speak of the grace of God, and as they were faithful to the Gospel, God Himself brought forth miraculous works giving witness to the message preached.

The lesson is a simple one. We are to seek God and Him only. When we do this, we actually release His power in our lives.

If you are willing to center your life in Jesus Christ and in the word of His grace, you will see the mighty power of God at work in you and through you like you've never seen it before. Our God is a jealous God, and He won't allow His children to place what He does before who He is. The gift must never become greater than the Giver. We have to be diligent concerning this. We must always watch our hearts. We need to make sure that our Christianity is not straying from Christ and instead being turned into a self centered religion which revolves around what we can get from God. Our Lord loves us too much to let us go down such a perilous road, and *we* must love Him enough to not let that happen.

Seek God for who He is. Love Him with all your heart, soul, mind, and strength. Learn to minister to Him not for what you can get out of Him, but for the simple reason that He deserves our praise. Stay in His grace at all times, and you will find He will not only meet all of your needs but He will "do exceedingly abundantly beyond all that we ask or think" (Ephesians 3:20).

God bears witness to His grace. We see this principle at work in the life of Stephen. Acts 6:8 says, "And Stephen, full of grace and power, was performing great wonders and signs among the people." You see, if you make it your job to stay fixed upon God's grace, you will become full and overflowing. As grace goes forth, the power of God will go along with it performing signs and wonders.

Again, you don't seek the wonders. They aren't conjured up by some great inner power you possess. You don't psyche yourself up to the point of being able to perform these things. You seek the Lord. You focus your full attention upon Him and *He* does the miracles through you.

I've heard many people ask the question about how healings can take place in a meeting where the minister is a known charlatan. They can't deny the great works which occur, but at the same time they are unable to reconcile this with the fact of the preacher being a fake. You see, the problem here is that they are naturally associating the miracles with the man instead of with the Lord. It seems when something great happens we think that the particular person through whom the wonder occurred is responsible for it. But man doesn't do it, God does.

The reason why so many great signs can take place in a meeting like this is because God is looking at the hearts and needs of the people there. The fact that some miracle occurs is not due to an individual, as we so often assume, but it is because God has seen a need in the hearts of someone seeking Him and He has chosen, by His grace, to meet that need. If one of my crusades is visited by the miracle working power of God, I'm not so arrogant as to think I must have been doing something right that day. I know God has looked upon the hearts of those who have come together, and I know that as we look to Him, He ministers out of His grace. I can't take the credit, and I don't want anybody giving me the credit. God does it. Every single time a miracle occurs it's because God chooses to do it, and not because some individual has brought it to pass.

We need to stop looking at individuals as if they are some type of supermen. We need to look unto Jesus in and for all things. He is our Source. He is the Giver of all good things. He is the One who performs all miracles.

Don't assume God will perform miracles through some spiritual dynamo but not through you. If that's the way you think, then you can't be looking at His grace. Make up your mind to be Christ-centered in all things. Speak and testify of the grace of God and you will find God will always confirm His grace in your life. If you seek the signs and wonders, you may never see them. But if you will seek the Lord and Him only with all your heart, I tell you He will give you more miracles than you ever dreamed possible. Stay in the word of His grace and He will bear witness to it, "granting that signs and wonders be done" in your life.

# Chapter 30

# Grace is Everywhere

*"Thus says the Lord, 'The people who survived the sword found grace in the wilderness-Israel, when it went to find its rest.' The Lord appeared to him from afar, saying, 'I have loved you with an everlasting love; therefore I have drawn you with lovingkindness.'"*                    *Jeremiah 31:2&3*

Grace is always there whenever you need it. If you're on top of the mountain, grace is there. If you're in the valley of the shadow of death, grace is there. God's grace is always sufficient for you and this means grace is always available to you, because grace, the essence of God, lives in you.

How this differs from much of Christianity. So often you find yourself directed inward by the many teachings existent today. Usually God's blessings are held at arms length. You are told they are there, and then you are exhorted to work and achieve so you can attain whatever particular blessing is being spoken of. The result of all this is that instead of looking to the Lord and His ample provision, you are put in a state of being aware only of your ability, or as the case many times turns out, your lack of ability.

How many Christians have given up because of this type of teaching? How many, after bitter tears and pain in their own continuing failures, have concluded that they will never have the blessing God's word speaks so often of? The sad truth is that there are thousands of believers who have found themselves in this state.

In my radio counselling ministry, one of the most frequent type of calls I receive comes from the sincere brother or sister in Christ who has been led to believe they will never have the abundant life Jesus spoke of. They accepted this wrong conclusion because, at their place of fellowship, they were fed a steady diet of works oriented Christianity. Sunday after Sunday they listened to sin centered messages, or self centered teachings, where everything depended upon their performance instead of upon the Lord. In this type of atmosphere the only thing produced is an ever deepening awareness of a person's own faults and weaknesses. So, these brothers and sisters are made to feel the preacher must be some spiritual giant, while they must be the poorest excuse of a Christian that ever lived.

How wrong this is. What a tragedy that this type of harmful and depriving teaching exists. In Jesus' ministry, the thrust of His teachings was always, "Come unto Me." God never intended for Jesus' death at Calvary to be merely an exhortation for people to work harder. He came to save. He saved us from sin and death and He saved us from our own efforts.

Don't you understand we are free in Him? Do you realize when Jesus said, "It is finished," that this statement was relevant for our whole lives and not just for our initial introduction into His kingdom? Our salvation is a complete salvation, one which covers all our lives, from the time we first say yes to Him to the time when we will finally go to be with Him.

I realize this may be a new thing to some of you. Perhaps you never heard this before and while you tremble at the excitement of this truth, you are nevertheless afraid to believe such a good thing could be real. All I can do is share with you what the Bible says. In this book I have endeavored to be as complete and honest with you as I can be concerning God's grace, and the fact is, grace is great news.

Grace frees us from the narrow confines of our own limited abilities. Grace frees us from our own meager understandings into the higher ways and thoughts of our Lord. Grace always points us to Jesus, because grace is Jesus. Grace tells us we are safe and secure in the arms of our Lord. Grace puts Christianity where it belongs, in Jesus Christ. Grace lets you be all you've ever wanted to be, because grace connects you with the power of God. Grace *is* your abundance, your victory, your strength, your obedience, your faith, hope, and love. Grace is the revelation of God to the world.

Grace is everywhere. No matter where you are, grace is there. Are you in some dark corner, away from the mainstream of God's life? Grace is there. Are you backslidden, caught up in what you thought would produce happiness for you? Grace is there. Is there some habitual sin that has become a monkey on your back? Grace is there. Has your heart become hardened through some tragedy in your life? Grace is there.

No matter what condition you are in, grace is there waiting for you. God has never required you to solve your own problems. All He asks is that you be willing to turn to Him and trust Him to be your salvation in all things. Perhaps you've heard the old adage, "You made your bed, now you must lie in it." Could it be you have believed this is God's attitude toward you? Nothing could be further from the truth. God takes no delight in your suffering. He is not waiting at the sidelines, watching your actions. His word is always, "Return to me, declares the Lord of hosts, that I may return to you" (Zechariah 1:3).

To be honest with you, I have found that the very thing which keeps many a Christian from going forward in the Lord is the fact that they really believe they have to work out their own problems. You sin, so you think it's up to you to take care of your sin. You backslide, so you think you have to undo everything by yourself before God will have anything to do with you. Or even worse, you may feel God will never have use for you ever again. Don't you see how these attitudes come from your defining God according to your principles and emotions rather than according to His word?

If you will be willing to return to Him today, and by that I mean a simple trust in His love and commitment to you and in you, you will find He has been there all along.

Jeremiah had this word from the Lord, "Thus says the Lord, 'The people who survived the sword found grace in the wilderness-Israel, when it went to find its rest.' The Lord appeared to him from afar, saying, 'I have loved you with an everlasting love; therefore I have drawn you with lovingkindness' " (31:2&3).

Israel had been cast into exile. They had lost their homeland, and this came as the result of their continual disobedience to the Lord. Yet God spoke to His people in terms of great unconditional love and tenderness. Significantly, the Word says they found grace in the wilderness. In other words, it doesn't matter where you are; grace is always there. God knew if there was one thing that would turn His people around, it would be grace. Even though they were in the wilderness, a barren and dry wasteland, there was still grace there.

Grace is like a message in a bottle to a shipwreck survivor on a deserted isle, and the message is, "You're not alone. I'm here too. I've loved you with an everlasting love." You may feel completely alone, apart from God and beyond help, but grace is there and if you will only turn to it you will hear the Lord saying, "I have drawn you with lovingkindness."

Grace is God's drawing power. He draws unbelievers to Himself through grace. He draws His own children closer and closer into Him with grace. Grace always says, "Come closer."

Don't be afraid. Don't look at yourself. Look at Him. Grace is everywhere. There is grace for you right now. Grace will always be with you all of your life. Grace will always bring you to Jesus. God's grace has invaded the world and the only reason the world doesn't see it is because it is too busy looking at itself.

Grace is true Cristianity. It doesn't matter where you are or where you have been. All that matters is that grace is there with you right now. Turn to it, looking unto Jesus, and you will discover grace has wrapped around you and is drawing you into God.

# Chapter 31

# I Am What I Am
# By the Grace of God

*"By the grace of God I am what I am, and His grace toward me did not prove vain; but I labored even more than all of them, yet not I, but the grace of God with me."*

*1st Corinthians 15:10*

I find it rather strange that the main argument raised against grace is the old excuse that if someone just lives in grace they will be lazy or they will run into sin and think it's not important. The people who say these things obviously have no idea what grace is. They think grace means only "unmerited favor." In other words, it's a concept to them. As far as they're concerned, grace isn't alive in the person of Jesus; it's only a doctrine to be considered and incorporated with all their other doctrines. With such an understanding as that, grace is bound to become diluted and ulti- mately made little more than a statement indicating how we were saved.

Isn't it peculiar that those in positions of ministry seem to be afraid of grace? Don't you find it odd to hear opinions expressed from the pulpit about grace that paint it as if it is a sin you indulge in rather than it being the very power of God?

In this book we've looked long and hard at God's grace. We've examined the Scriptures together and I find nothing in the Bible which supports the narrow minded arguments being voiced against grace. Instead I have found that walking in grace is truly the walk of faith because in grace I am trusting 100% in God's power and not in my ability at all. In grace we walk according to the mind of Christ, realizing the folly of our own thoughts.

Grace is supremely relevant to every aspect of our Christian life. There is not one thing we need which we cannot find in the grace of God. As we saw earlier, grace upon grace is the fullness of God (John 1:16).

Think about what those who criticize grace say, and compare that to what Paul the Apostle wrote about himself in his first letter to the Corinthian church. He said, "By the grace of God I am what I am, and His grace toward me did not prove vain; but I labored even more than all of them, yet not I, but the grace of God with me" (15:10).

The "all of them" Paul referred to were all the other apostles combined. He said he labored more than all of them put together. You certainly do receive this impression as you read the New Testament. Who founded the churches in Asia Minor? Paul did. Who began the churches in Greece? Paul did. Who had the desire to preach the Gospel in the uttermost parts of the known world; Spain? Paul did. Who endured the most sufferings and persecutions? Paul did.

Paul was not bragging when he said he labored more than all of them, he was merely stating the fact, and the point he was specifically making was that his labor was not the product of his own will-power, but it was produced by the grace of God. God's grace made Paul who he was.

How can anyone say a grace only consciousness will produce lazy and sinful believers? If there is any sin to be found in that accusation, I'm afraid those who slander the grace of God would be the guilty party.

Let me tell you something about what happens when grace touches your life. Grace is the personification of the love of God meeting you where you are. God's grace has made me who I am, and nobody will ever be able to say I'm a lazy Christian or one who sins and doesn't care. These are mere prejudices which those who have no understanding voice in order to justify their own continuance in a works and self centered religion. My life is dedicated to the Lord. I have been bought with a price and I know I am no longer my own. I belong to Jesus Christ and I exist to serve Him. My life in this time and space environment is spent ministering to my Lord Jesus and ministering the Gospel to the world at large. I labor diligently, not to earn a thing from God, but because He has given me so much. The love He has showered upon me has created a new heart. I was lost and now I am found. I was blind and now I see. His amazing grace has produced in me the desire to serve Him all the days of my life and it is not by power or by might but by His Spirit that I can do all things. Grace has made real the declaration, "Christ in you, the hope of glory" (Colossians 1:27).

When you allow God's grace to have its way in your life, you realize you are exactly the person God has made you to be. Your searching and striving end, as you see yourself perfect and complete in Him.

Paul labored more than all of them, and as he said, "yet not I, but the grace of God with me."

You can hear a lot about the importance of resting in the Lord. "Faith-rest" is a term commonly used. Well, this verse tells you what a real faith rest is all about. When you trust in the finished work of Jesus Christ, you can really rest. This doesn't mean you never do anything. What it means is that you recognize what God has done, and whatever you do is a result and product of His accomplishment. Grace is true spiritual rest because grace puts you in the realm of God's power working within you. You can labor more than all of them too, but if you do it in grace you will be able to say, "yet not I, but the grace of God within me."

Paul summed up his entire life in saying, "By the grace of God I am what I am." Can you say the same thing about yourself? The fact is, whether you believe it or not, it's still true for you. You may think there are some things you've done by your own power, but I tell you anything you've done in the name of Christ has come about as a result of grace. There are many believers who take a certain pride in where they have come in their growth in God. They are mistaken. They have not produced one iota of spiritual life. God has done it all by His grace. You may not know it but you are what you are by the grace of God.

We have seen so much together in this book. In this closing chapter I truly pray these words are absolute reality to you. My desire is for you to be filled with all the fullness of God. I hope you can say, "I am what I am by the grace of God" and realize what a powerful and complete statement this is. God's grace, the essence of Jesus, is our salvation, our growth, our victory, our everything we need in this life.

There will always be those who argue against grace. Don't let their words dissuade you from what you know to be true. They may criticize you and accuse you as you choose to walk by faith and not by sight. You may even become a spiritual outcast at their hands. But remember, you are what you are by the grace of God. When you are met with judgment and condemnation, return a blessing. Think about the time when you too didn't know what the real meaning of grace was. Extend grace to those who may oppose you and perhaps the manifestation of God's love and grace coming from you will shine a light into their darkness.

God has sent His son, Jesus Christ, into the world to draw all men unto Him. Many respond, and sadly many don't. To those who do, Jesus becomes their Savior and Lord. Beyond this point His call to us is to be conformed into His image. Many respond, and sadly many don't. To those who do, Jesus becomes their very breath and life. Beyond this point His call to us is to be what we are by the grace of God. Many respond, and I trust you have as well. Go now, and live in the fullness of God's grace.

# Appendix

Listed below are some materials we feel will be of help to you in a further understanding of this important issue. The tapes and literature are available through Loving Grace Ministries, Box 531, Lancaster, NH 03584. All contributions will be used to reach out with the Gospel.

**SINGLE CASSETTE TAPES BY WAYNE MONBLEAU**
**$5.00 each**
These tapes are either 60 or 90 minutes long and carry a lifetime guarantee on sound quality.

**WHO ARE YOU LISTENING TO?**                    **LGT 123**
A scriptural analysis of the great difference between law and grace, and a compelling argument for walking in total grace.

**COMING INTO TRUE FREEDOM**                    **LGT 901**
A special 90 minute tape of an anointed crusade Wayne held in New York. This tape will challenge you to walk in real freedom.

**GRACE AND THE LAW**                    **LGT 130**
Taken from the books of Romans and Hebrews, Wayne teaches in a direct and clear cut manner the triumph of God's grace over the law.

## A COMPLETE TRUST IN THE NEW COVENANT, AND WHY THE LAW PRODUCES FAILURE               LGT 179

Starting in the old testament, Wayne reveals the ultimate purpose of the law; to be written on our hearts through the fulfillment of Messiah. Consequently, those who still try to fulfill the law today are depriving themselves of the new covenant. An excellent study tape.

## GRACE PRODUCES OBEDIENCE               LGT 187

Those who criticize grace claim it causes laziness and gives people a license to sin. Wayne explores these myths in this dynamic series of messages on the motivating power of grace in our lives.

## MY TESTIMONY               LGT 152

Wayne shares how he came to know Jesus Christ in this 90 minute special tape of his first crusade in Philadelphia.

## GRACE!               LGT 176, 177, 178

The 16 meditations in this series have been selected over a 2½ year period from Wayne's live messages over the "Let's Talk About Jesus" radio program. You won't find a finer, more in depth, and inspirational series on grace anywhere else.

Titles: Grace is stronger than sin; Grace is a gift; The throne of grace; Justified by grace; Falling from grace; The fullness of grace; 4 exhortations concerning grace; The definition of grace; Paul's testimony of grace; God's wisdom is grace; Grace upon grace; Freedom from sin; Liberty with wisdom; A character study of grace; Be strong in God's grace. 3 tape series $13.00.

# OTHER LITERATURE BY WAYNE MONBLEAU

## FRIENDSHIP WITH GOD
Already on its way to becoming a classic in Christian literature, this book brings you into an awareness of your own uniquely close relationship with the Lord. In Wayne's lucid way of explaining Scripture, he shares from his life experience and opens the Bible up to us concerning enjoying a friendship with God. A compelling book which you'll want to read again and again.

Single copy - $3.95

Bulk - 10 copies - $29.95

## A HOME BIBLE STUDY COURSE ON THE GRACE OF GOD
### By Wayne Monbleau

## THE GRACE OF GOD
This twelve lesson home study course is designed to give the student a well rounded understanding of the grace of God, and at the same time it encourages him to develop insight into the word of God. Lessons consist of 12 teachings on cassette tape, to be completed one per week, along with two companion books. Each lesson has a number of questions. Some are essay; others are word studies, and all require the student to be digging into the Bible. Each assignment is mailed to our main office, is gone over by a staff instructor, and is returned with comments, every fourth week. Write us for information regarding the start of the next semester.

Tuition - $85

------------ CLIP OUT AND SEND IN ------

## Loving Grace Ministries
### P.O. BOX 531
### LANCASTER, N.H. 03584

☐ *Yes, I'm interested in taking the Grace of God Bible study course. Please let me know when the next semester begins.*

☐ *Enclosed is my check for $85. Enroll me now. I want to be sure I'm in the next class.*

☐ *Please send me your complete tape, record and literature lists.*

| QUAN. | NO. | TITLE | EACH | TOTAL |
|-------|-----|-------|------|-------|
|       |     |       |      |       |
|       |     |       |      |       |
|       |     |       |      |       |
|       |     |       |      |       |
|       |     |       |      |       |
|       |     |       |      |       |
|       |     | **TOTAL ENCLOSED** | | $ |

**NAME**

**ADDRESS**

**CITY**          **STATE**          **ZIP**

### Allow 3 Weeks For Delivery

**Additional Copies of this Book
May be Ordered from**

*Loving Grace Publications*

**BOX 531
LANCASTER, NH 03584**

Single copy — $5.95
Bulk offer - ten copies $49.95 — $4.99 per copy

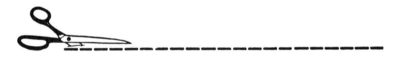

PLEASE SEND ME _____ MORE COPIES OF
YOUR BOOK "GRACE - The essence of God."

I HAVE ENCLOSED $_____ TO COVER THE COST.

_____

NAME
_____

ADDRESS
_____

CITY                    STATE              ZIP

Allow 3 Weeks For Delivery